How to Turn
a Passion for Food
into Profit

BOOKS BY JEANNE A. VOLTZ

The California Cookbook
The L.A. Gourmet (with Burks Hamner)
The Los Angeles Times Natural Foods Cookbook
The Flavor of the South

How to Turn a Passion for Food into Profit

ELAYNE J. KLEEMAN
and JEANNE A. VOLTZ

RAWSON, WADE PUBLISHERS, INC.
New York

ISBN: 89256–086–X
LCCN: 78–64800

Library of Congress Cataloging in Publication Data

Kleeman, Elayne J
   How to turn a passion for food into profit.

   Includes index.
   1. Food service—Vocational guidance.
2. Cookery—Vocational guidance.   3. Restaurants,
lunch rooms, etc.—Vocational guidance.   I. Voltz,
Jeanne, joint author.   II. Title.
TX911.2.K54   641′.023   78-64800
ISBN 0-89256-086-X

Composition by American–Stratford Graphic Services, Inc.,
Brattleboro, Vermont
Printed and bound by Fairfield Graphics, Fairfield, Pennsylvania

Designed by A. Christopher Simon
First Edition

for Les Dames d'Escoffier of New York City

Acknowledgments

We wish to thank the dozens of men and women who generously shared their experiences and advice to beginners in businesses involved with cooking, but it is impossible to name them all. Most are credited with their remarks in the body of the book. Special thanks are due:

Ken McKenna, a veteran newspaperman, and now feature writer with *The New York Daily News*, who assisted with writing and research on the business chapter.

Rocco Angelo, associate professor in the school of hotel, food, and travel services, Florida International University, Miami, for suggesting points of expansion to assist the reader in the restaurant chapter.

Stella Dratler, Jack Lynes, Michael Demarest, Ruth Ellen Church, William Rice, Marietta Marcin, and Frances Ellen Paul for sharing their knowledge and assisting in locating successful amateurs gone professional.

Marjorie Szymona for countless hours putting copy script into neatly typed manuscript form and giving a reader's appraisal while she was at the job.

Contents

How to Turn
a Passion for Food
into Profit

Chapter 1

Who's a Candidate
for Cooking Success?

Who would give up the security of an orderly life as a stockbroker, ad copywriter, housewife, or almost any other occupation for the uncertainty of a career in cooking? After interviewing scores of people who've done it, most of them with a great sense of accomplishment, we think they're pretty special.

They're creative, and many of these cooking professionals have had a nagging feeling that they wanted to get out of mundane ruts. They wanted something more than a nine-to-five professional routine or spic-and-span houses and well-scrubbed children.

Most of them love the feel, the smell, of fresh good food, the looks of a beautiful dish, and the trappings that go with serving or cooking it or purchasing it. They respond to appreciative gastronomes as a Barrymore or Carol Channing responds to a theater audience or a Michener responds to seeing his name on best-seller lists for months at a time.

They have other gifts—a good head for a business, a

3

way with words or sentences, or a knack for genuine hospitality or teaching—to help them put their love affairs with cooking to work.

They are gluttons for work. But really, do professionals in the food business work any harder than dedicated workers in other fields?

Almost any career you can think of is represented among the food professionals and business people we interviewed. One restaurateur was a jazz musician. One caterer was a high school science teacher, and another, an ad copywriter. Students work in restaurants or food sales to put themselves through universities, then find themselves operating the restaurants. One student helped put her husband through an engineering course at a university by selling fruitcakes. The business was so good that her husband abandoned thoughts of finishing college and decided to help her sell fruitcakes instead.

Dozens of caterers, gourmet shop operators, food writers, restaurateurs, and dessert and quiche bakers were full-time housewives before they went into business, wrote their first articles for sale, or brought home their first paychecks. The organizational ability that keeps a household running smoothly can be applied to business by the person with enough drive to try.

Cecile Lamalle Woicik considers herself the epitome of a woman who had to "do something," and she knew early on that her interest was cooking. "I was a professional housewife for seventeen years," she says, "but always with the thought nagging at me that I needed something more." She eventually took courses in hotel and restaurant cooking at New York City Community College, worked in a restaurant kitchen, wrote articles for magazines, operated a cookware and gift shop at the family's country place, and taught cooking. She now is food editor of a restaurant trade magazine, and thinks her career still is evolving. "I can never be a full-time housewife again," she adds.

Nathalie Dupree, director of a cooking school at Rich's Department Store in Atlanta, advises the restless person with a yen to cook to try it. "A restaurant here hires people for a few hours a week, teaches them to make just one or two dishes," she says. "The pay isn't much, but you find out right away if you really want to go into food as a career. And the opportunity is there if you do."

Mrs. Dupree herself operated a French restaurant in Social Circle, Georgia, an hour's drive from Atlanta, and carried a morning paper route and lived in a trailer to support herself while she was building her restaurant business. It was a grueling life for a few years, but worth it to have the restaurant she wanted.

Actors gravitate to food, partly because it is a handy part-time job between engagements, but also because showmanship is an element in food presentation. James Beard, the jovial picture of a man who sprang to life eating, cooking, talking, and writing about food, was an aspiring actor before he fell into food almost by blind chance, first assisting friends in an hors d'oeuvre catering business, then writing about hors d'oeuvre, then opening his famous cooking school. The late Michael Field was a concert pianist before he became a cooking school director and food writer.

A few non-cooks have made a profession of their interest in food. Ira Horowitz, a film editor for several years, doesn't cook at all, but opened a gourmet food shop in the Murray Hill section of New York City, hired a cook, and within a year expanded his kitchen and was looking forward to opening a restaurant in conjunction with his shop.

The first obstacle may be convincing your family, friends, and customers that you're serious about cooking for profit. Customers may be reluctant to buy if you can't guarantee stocks six months later for reordering; this is especially true in the manufacturing of fancy food items. Your family and friends are likely to expect that your time is still their time—until you get a sale so big you have to push other responsibilities aside.

If you're serious, you can do it, as the people we have interviewed prove. If you want a little part-time job, even that works in some cases. Any way you can go at it, cooking is fun—and can be profitable.

So you're not exactly Julia Child! Neither was she the great cook and TV chef at one time. When she and Paul Child were married after World War II, she had no special interest in cooking. To please her husband, who was assigned to the U.S. embassy in Paris, she took lessons at l'Académie Cordon Bleu, was invited to a women's gastronomical society by Simca (Simone Beck) where she met Louisette Bertholle. The three women opened a small cooking school in Paris at the request of American friends, wrote a book that was on the best-seller list for weeks— and Mrs. Child, the former non-cook, became one of the best-known women cooks in the world.

"Certainly cooking is one of the very best ways of making money," Mrs. Child wrote us, "since there are so many things one can do, from teaching to catering to having a home bakeshop."

Career-switching has become a minor fad of the times. Children go off to school, and mothers are left at loose ends. Men feel trapped in a rat race or a nine-to-five routine that gives them the blahs. Young adults, in mid college, after, or without college, cast about for something more satisfying to fill their lives than the slots they fell into or were chosen for them by parents or teachers. These folk are looking for exciting new careers, creative, absorbing, and, incidentally, profitable.

Thousands of these restless women, men, and teenagers with a passion for cooking, or at least a great dish or dessert in their culinary repertoires, have untapped salable skills they don't suspect. These cooking fanatics can make extra dollars, in some cases handsome livings, with their culinary skills. Hundreds of good home cooks have proven they can go professional, and we'll tell you the success stories of many of them. Nothing adds zest to cooking—the most creative of everyday jobs—more than having an appreciative audience, especially one that pays for the creativity.

Cooking for profit offers special benefits to the individual. You can be your own boss—setting your hours, accepting as much or as little work as you choose, hiring and firing people to help, and buying equipment, maybe something you've deprived yourself of for years, but now can afford as a business expense. It's not all fun and games, for along with the joys of being your own boss, you have the headaches, the potential losses, the labor market, and the capricious tastes of customers to contend with.

Examine your qualifications honestly and fairly. Do you like to cook? Do you like cooking enough to be stuck with it when the latest novel or lunch out or other pastime beckons? If you become a professional, there will be times when you'd rather play than cook. Do you do at least one cooking job *really* well? To be marketable, home cooking must be unique, better than commercial products on the market, or you cannot compete. Decide what special dish or service you want to sell. Ask yourself if you can dedicate yourself to it as a career. Your grandma's fruitcake that you enjoy baking so much, and all your friends urge you to put on the market, might become a cruel chore after you've prepared five hundred of them. You can learn to hate the very smell of it.

Is there a market for your food or service, and at a price that allows you a profit? Chapter 2 discusses in detail getting into business and making a go of it, but before you turn to the services of an attorney, accountant, and other professional help you must be honest with yourself. Will people buy the food you think is so unique? Will they pay enough for it to make it worthwhile for you?

How much time will your hobby/career cooking take, and do you have the time to devote to it as a money-making project? A cooking school can be started at home, and a few communities allow cooking for sale at home if kitchens are brought up to commercial standards. If you can work at home, you may not have to arrange for babysitters or other household help. Or you may need extra help for cooking and packaging and selling a cookery craft. Is the help available in your area?

Is the food or service seasonal? Does the busy season slack off for your vacation and personal busy times or does it conflict with them? If you choose a mail-order business that becomes hectic in October and November, can you dovetail your holiday preparations around packing and shipping customers' candies or cheese gift boxes? If you must depend on fruits and vegetables in season for relishes or jams, are you willing to give up lazy days at the beach for time over a steamy stove?

There are at least two dozen ways we, and successful entrepreneurs before you, have devised for you to make money from a talent in the kitchen. We'll suggest how to get started, where to look for markets, and how to individualize your foods or services, plus ideas for smart planning to avoid the pitfalls and nasty little surprises that afflict novices. We'll tell you how to be a businessperson without becoming a hardhearted wheeler and dealer.

We'll help you get a price and stick with it or adjust to changing costs and markets. A cake is a cake is a cake, and you pay for butter, eggs, sugar, nuts, and fruits that go into it, plus the wrapping and transportation to the customer. Add the cost of your time and talent, a percentage for profit, and you have your price. We will suggest ways to use the labor market available, fairly and squarely, even in the smallest communities where neighbors constitute the main and practically only labor force. We hope we give you the guidance to help you hire wisely and the courage to fire an employee who is a misfit.

There are many reasons why you want to and should go into the cooking business—you're at mid-life, feeling unfulfilled in your nine-to-five rut. You're widowed or divorced and need a restorative for your self-esteem. Or you need an exciting sideline job to supplement your income, and many food-involved businesses can be practiced part-time. Or you're plain bored with your work, yourself, and life. You'll find a half dozen or more successful culinary entrepreneurs in the following chapters who left good, supposedly glamorous, jobs for the creative adventure of food businesses. An ad copywriter just might think catering is more fulfilling, and one did, ultimately with great success.

If you're reentering the job market or switching from brainy work to handiwork, get in the kitchen, where you feel more at home than at one of the typewriters invented since you left the office routine. You can tackle cooking for profit at any age and in any city, town, or village. You don't need a degree in food technology, culinary arts, home economics, or food service, though any of them can help and we will tell you where to go for education, if you want more. You just need a deft hand for a culinary specialty or group of specialties and a reasonably good head for business or the sense to ask for business help.

Accent the positive—your very best food or the best
meal you prepare—and with any luck at all you'll make
money and enjoy every minute of it. Even those late
nights adding receipts can be a pleasure, especially if the
receipts come out ahead of the debits.

Chapter 2

What It Takes to Start

Usually, it happens almost accidentally. A dinner guest remarks on the absolute perfection of a dessert. "If you could package that," he nods at his empty plate, "you'd make a million dollars."

You smile at the compliment and think, *I wonder . . .*

At a dinner party a friend chats with you in the kitchen as you are preparing the next course. She watches in awe as you, apron over dinner dress, casually spoon out a delicate soufflé for eighteen guests. "You're a pro in the kitchen," she observes.

You look at her and think, *She's right. I am!*

Okay, you are convinced that you are dynamite at the oven. How do you start selling your cooking creations? How do you go into business? The move can be complicated or simple, slow or fast, costly or cheap, all depending on your abilities and the route you select to utilize them. Cooking for profit should be a natural extension of a cook's or baker's natural inclinations. And there are abundant examples of amateur cooks who once thought

11

only of pleasing their families and now are pleasing hundreds of thousands of customers.

Look at Mrs. Irma Groff. She and her family started Groff's Farm Restaurant, a landmark of good eating in the Pennsylvania-Dutch country of eastern Pennsylvania. Mrs. Groff was a young housewife with a small child when she felt stirred to do something else. Housework did not fully occupy her anymore, and she and her husband could use the extra money. She toyed with the idea of getting a part-time job in the local bank. Her family objected. There was a child to bring up.

She cast about for alternatives. Her chief talents were in the kitchen. She decided to open a restaurant for the tourists who crowded the roads much of the year to view the picturesque Amish farmers. From her experience with town social events, she felt competent to handle large groups. Hers was a working dairy farm, fresh ingredients were handy, and the ample farmhouse living room would serve as a dining hall. Besides, she enjoyed cooking. Over the years, the restaurant has thrived and won praise from such cooking notables as James Beard and Craig Claiborne.

Ellie Siegel's home looks out at another apartment house on the Upper East Side of Manhattan, not the lush rolling hills of Pennsylvania farmland. But she had the same cooking urge a few years ago. She knew she was a gifted baker. She had been complimented enough times, and she had some marvelous recipes from her European mother. Her husband kept nagging at her to work, not so much for the money as to keep her active now that their three young children were in school all day.

She heard about a specialty store opening in the neighborhood. The next morning she presented the proprietor with twenty-four freshly baked brownies. They sold out during the lunch hour. In six months, she had extended her repertoire to fruit tarts and quiches and was selling to other stores. Friends began ordering desserts from her when they were having parties. Soon she was working with a caterer and earning $250 a week while still baking at home and taking care of her family.

One warning: Ellie Siegel (not her real name) is breaking the law. Food handling is subject to many controls, the Federal Food, Drug and Cosmetics Act, and cooking at home for outside consumption lies beyond the reach of regulation. The federal statutes are complemented by an array of state laws and local health regulations. Mrs. Siegel is one of a growing corps of women who practice closet cuisine for profit. They are bootlegging products to specialty stores, restaurants, caterers—to any food seller looking for individually prepared goods. The practice cannot be condoned but it does exist (more later).

Economic factors such as higher personal income have fueled interest among the public for the more expensive types of food that come out of the home kitchen, a taste revolt against the homogenized commercial food of today. But a number of sociological changes have occurred in the 1970s that have turned the business of food preparation into a bull market. Americans are dining out more than ever before and have been since 1970, spurred, for one thing, by the high cost of supermarket food. They now spend 28 percent of their food dollar in eating and drinking places, according to a 1977 survey by *Sales and Market Management* magazine.

The surge of women going out to work is one of the major reasons for the rise in restaurant dining, but this phenomenon also has affected other food services. Women on the job all day have no time to prepare elaborate meals. They depend more and more on caterers for everything from party dinners to weekend teas and cocktail parties. The vacation home trend has opened new markets for caterers and other food services in areas where sociability is a way of life. In the suburbs, as affluent and outgoing as ever, busy hostesses are depending increasingly on outside food preparers.

The young, so-called singles set represents another market that has little patience with sweating in the kitchen. They eat out more than any other age group and have been educated to casual, rather exotic dining. Even married persons in their twenties and thirties, influenced by women's liberation and tending to small families, regard such household chores as cookery as a drudgery from which to escape. Admittedly, cooking as a hobby is blossoming, as Julia Child has commented, but that's for occasional fun, not as a way of life. And kitchen experimentation has sharpened the public appetite for fancy foods from the home oven.

Still, if you want to start your own business, there are some fundamental standards that your prospective enterprise should meet before you concern yourself with money, licensing, insurance, and the scores of other considerations that later will nag at you. Ask yourself:

· Does your product or service satisfy a public need or desire?
· Does your operation have some potential for expansion?
· Does your product or service have a claim to individuality?
· Do you know your competition, their strengths and weaknesses?

The first criterion is covered in the discussion of the popularity of home-prepared foods. A lively market does exist for almost anything you do with food on a personal basis, from restaurants and specialty stores to caterers and cooking schools.

Secondly, the potential for expansion is there in spades; given the right idea, it is virtually limitless. The food industry remains one of the few in the country in which the individual entrepreneur can not only thrive but prosper mightily. Some of today's great private fortunes are based on fresh ideas for the processing or selling of food.

Maurice and Richard McDonald, after all, were transplanted New Englanders who started a hamburger shop in San Bernardino, California, after World War II. Their gimmick was simplicity itself. Cheap food, carefully cooked, and fast, no-frills service. When Ray Kroc, now board chairman, bought the right to franchise the hamburger stores, he was a fifty-two-year-old paper-cup salesman. Through the 1960s, he pioneered the fast-food concept, and today the vast McDonald's chain grosses more than $1 billion a year.

McDonald's went a step further than scoring a whopping financial success. As Paul D. Paganucci, associate dean at Dartmouth's Amos Tuck School of Business Administration, has pointed out, the chain "revolutionized an entire food service industry, changing eating habits throughout the world, and raised customer expectations."

Anyone who has bitten into a Big Mac might quarrel with the second half of the professor's statement but the McDonald story demonstrates that a person with a different approach to serving or selling food can make an enormous business triumph. Along the way, he or she could alter the way Americans eat.

In cooking services, uniqueness can be an operation's readiest ingredient. The quality of the product—a blueberry pie that tastes divine, a pastry that melts in your mouth—may be incomparable. Or you may have a little-known method of preparing foods that will catch the public fancy.

In a survey of small business, the magazine *U.S. News & World Report* interviewed two Atlanta women whose restaurant featured sandwiches made with whole-wheat bread cooked in pottery flowerpots. In four years, the women, Mrs. Jane Nichols, and her daughter, Sally, were running three Atlanta eateries with total sales of more than $500,000 a year. In New York City, Manganaro's, an Italian food store, overcame its poor location on Manhattan's grubby midtown West Side when its owners dreamed up the idea of selling outsize hero sandwiches, a dozen or more feet long. The jumbos became the rage at chic uptown East Side parties.

Mark McNeely, twenty-seven, copied no one when he opened his retail shop in California a few years ago. He had moved there after completing a business course at Harvard University. With these credentials and $5,000 of his own, he persuaded a bank to give him a $25,000 loan. He located a former music store in the small town of Hermosa Beach, remodeled it, and called his shop Just Desserts.

The menu was limited, featuring frozen yogurt, baked goods, and ice cream and later such creative dishes as mixed toffee bars, banana chips, and raisins in ice cream. The innovations were inspired enough to attract an expanding clientele. The bearded, smiling McNeely exulted, "People come from all over to try it." By 1978, he was employing eleven persons and was making plans to open a branch within a short drive of the campus of the University of California at Los Angeles. McNeely had analyzed his market as young people, like himself, and is catering to it. He even employs mostly teenagers. He explained his formula: "Find a little niche and fill it."

In the home-cooking business, one is rarely faced with direct competition from another person offering the same foods. If it happens, the deciding factor, in most instances, will be the quality of the product. Your customers—restaurants, supermarkets, specialty stores—are buying your pies, pastries, relishes, to enhance their appeal to the public. Home-produced products can give the restaurant a homelike atmosphere, the supermarket a feature no other store has, and the specialty store individuality. Price is not usually the overriding concern. Commercial producers can offer far lower prices than you, and that's their strength. Their weakness is the blandness of their products. The fundamental strength of homemade goods is that they cannot be duplicated in commercial ovens.

Cooking schools, too, are almost immune to competition; their popularity depends on the competence of the teachers. Other food services are not so fortunate. Restaurants and specialty stores must be wary of competitors as would any other retailer, careful always of their choice of location, types of food, and quality of service. Caterers have multiplied in urban areas in recent years, and the competition can be bitter. Here the quest for uniqueness has reached dizzying heights. Two New York City entries in the field are La Difference, with "continental glatt kosher cuisine," and the Rock Soul Food & West Indian Home Cooking in Brooklyn's Crown Heights.

Competition, the opportunity for expansion are standards by which the potential success of any enterprise can be judged. But small businesses, and cooking services in particular, have some personal criteria that also must be considered. There is one basic question that a person who wants to cook for profit must ask himself or herself: Do you genuinely like to prepare food and are you willing to spend dreary hours in the kitchen or in a store or restaurant? Almost any aspect of the food-service field is harshly demanding in time. Ellie Siegel, the Manhattan food baker, shrugs off fifteen- or sixteen-hour days. Jane Nichols and her daughter, who run the Atlanta restaurant Good Ol' Days, often work six days a week, sometimes from early morning to after midnight. They do everything themselves, from cooking to promotion. Yet the daughter can say, "I believe in doing something you enjoy. You just have got to want it bad enough." The hours are almost always long and the days off few, particularly in a business's first crucial years. Two young girls who started a specialty store in New York City had four days off during an eight-month period. Some new entrepreneurs reconcile themselves to never taking a vacation.

In the food-services line, the timing, too, is terrible. People entertain in the evenings, on weekends, on holidays. If you are in a resort area, acclimate yourself to spending summers in the kitchen and make do with Mondays and Tuesdays as "weekends." Remember, it's a long winter. People do seem to pick the most inconvenient times to throw a party. Ellie Siegel worked a dinner party on her husband's fiftieth birthday but made more than enough money to take him to a splendid restaurant the next night.

The homebound cook or baker must be extremely selfish; business and your needs as a business person come first. Barbara Dunn, the owner of a small business in San Francisco, described her attitude to a seminar on running a small business this way: "Something is going to give but it is not going to be me. There are days early in the business when the beds don't get made." The household routine must be built around the periods in which you are occupied, whether you work out of your home or spend endless hours in your restaurant or whatever.

Versatility

The single most prominent characteristic of the successful small-business man or woman is versatility. Big
corporations can afford layers of executives, each with his
tidy sphere of responsibility. In a small operation, the
owner might be called on to function as buyer, labor relations specialist, salesperson, and even, at times, delivery
person. Run down your personal pluses and minuses. We
assume you're a good cook or you would not be trying to
sell your wares for a profit. Perhaps you are shy and
would find it immensely difficult to peddle your own
goods. Ellie Siegel has the perfect personality for the
lone entrepreneur. "I have a big mouth," she said. "My
first customer, a store, I went to him and said, 'I hear
you're looking for someone to bake for you. I'm good. I'm
going to bake for you.'" Not everyone can perform like
that. Or you realize that the store or restaurant you are
contemplating is beyond your capacity as manager, or
you know you would not make a good dining room host;
you'd rather oversee the kitchen and the accounts. Then
you should consider a partner, someone who would com-
plement your abilities. But find an associate before you
proceed with your plans. A compatible partner is a rare
commodity.

Family-run operations probably are the most common
in small business. Members of the family divide up the
jobs to their own liking and abilities. The Barricinis
started a family candy store in New York City in 1930
and built it to a peak of thirty stores in the metropolitan
area. Two brothers manufactured the candy while their
wives took care of the store. Pizza Hut, a flourishing
worldwide fast-food chain, grew out of a family grocery
store and was started by two brothers with money supplied by their mother.

Now on to the nitty-gritty items—finance, bookkeeping,

laws and regulations, insurance—that frighten the novice businessman but need not. Remember, for every complex area of business life, there are professional counselors to guide you.

Financing a Business

All right, you have an idea for starting a business. Now you must ascertain how practical it is. Get out a pencil and paper. What will be your fixed costs, that is, costs that stay with you month to month? Rent. Labor. Utilities and telephone. Taxes. Interest charges (if you must borrow). Insurance premiums. Licensing fees. And salaries, including your own. Some experts hold that in a shoestring operation, the owner need not budget for himself initially or at least begin by paying himself very little. Whether valid or not, it should be a short-term situation.

Variable costs depend on volume. The higher the sales, the more materials you need, the more labor it will take, and a hodgepodge of ancillary expenses ranging from transportation to packaging. You are listing all the extra expenses that this business will cost. If you work out of your home, the added costs sometimes are elusive, but they are there.

Now make out a simple budget or earnings prospective, that is, an estimate of the expenses, sales, and profits that you expect to result from all business transactions over a certain period. Experts say a two-year plan is best. You figure the cost of materials, the expenses involved, and the potential sales and the amount of money they will bring in.

Decide on how much cash you need to start this business and how much you have or can borrow. One business adviser said, "People have only a sketchy idea of the amount of money involved in going into business. They fail to realize that they need subsistence from a source other than the business to carry them through the first two or three years."

In small operations, such as caterers or food schools, where little capital is required, the family and friends willing to invest for a percentage of the profits are a prime source for loans. If you go to professional lenders, be prepared to present a cash budget forecast and a schedule for repaying the loan from cash income. The bank's main criterion for lending money is your ability to pay it back.

A commercial bank or savings and loan association requires rather detailed information for a loan to a store. Its lending officer will want to know the cost of the fixtures and equipment, starting inventories, and a list of unexpected costs like deposits for utilities and fees for license permits.

A banker can be one of your most trusted counselors. It is his job to entertain propositions that bring profits into the bank through wise investment of its money. He should be viewed as a friend, not an antagonist. He profits from your success and loses when you fail. He will have sound advice. He is an expert in estimating fixed operating costs, capital needs, and the amount of money needed to start a business.

In a prosperous country like the United States, there are many sources of money for sound business ventures. Check the small-business investment companies in your area. The Small Business Administration has field offices throughout the country and makes loans at relatively low rates of interest. They will help small firms to finance expansion, purchase supplies and equipment, and acquire working capital.

Bringing in a partner might be the answer. If he is willing to invest the money, you will have the side benefit of having someone to share the worry and the work load with. That was the solution for Jane Wilson when her Party Box catering service ran into trouble. Jeff Perlman joined the firm, then five years old, in 1972, investing $5,000. The enterprise has been thriving ever since.

The amount of money you have to invest and a sound financial plan are crucial to your success, but there are exceptions. It may take months, or a year or two, to start a business. Dorothy McNett, who teaches microwave cooking and operates a store, Microwave 'N' Things, in Sunnyvale, California, plunged into business a little more than a month after coming up with the idea. She had no problems. "If your idea is good enough, you can take more of a risk," she said.

With about $250 for legal fees and licensing and $1,500 for stock and leasing a store—some her money, the rest borrowed—she opened her store—and succeeded. Her idea of combining sales and instruction in the use of microwave ovens was right for the time—early in the microwave boom. She started with no full-time employees so did not have to allocate capital for meeting a payroll, but four years later had a full-time professional on her staff and had opened a second store in nearby Redwood City.

When Frank and Dan Carney borrowed $600 to open Wichita's first pizza restaurant in 1958, they were not sure what they were doing for months. They had never seen or tasted pizza. Even the store's name was haphazard. The brothers called it Pizza Hut to fit the existing sign, which had room for only nine spaces, and five of them had to be "pizza." By the year's end, they were grossing $1,000 a week and the next year began franchising new outlets. Today Pizza Hut is the largest pizza restaurant system in the world, with 3,600 units in the United States and thirteen foreign countries. One Pizza Hut restaurant is located in a three-hundred-year-old building hard by the royal residence of the Netherlands in The Hague.

The Pizza Hut story is instructive in showing the odd ways in which money-making ideas surface and are put to practical use. The Carney brothers' family ran a neighborhood grocery store in Wichita. Dan, twenty-five, was taking his master's degree in business administration at Wichita State University. Frank, nineteen, was an undergraduate headed toward a degree in electrical engineering. Both brothers worked evenings and weekends at the grocery store.

The store's landlady owned a nearby building that housed a rowdy saloon, and she was constantly bothered by complaints about the noise. She decided to get rid of her troublesome tenants and approached the Carney brothers about opening a pizza shop there. She had read an article in the *Saturday Evening Post* about the popularity of the Italian snack food. "She wanted a neighborhood business to occupy her building," Frank recalled. "Although pizza was relatively unknown in Wichita at the time, we decided that it just might work." Then along came an airman from a nearby military base looking for part-time work. With the large Carney family peopling the store, there was little chance. But in the course of conversation, the airman, John Bender, mentioned that he once worked as a pizza cook in a restaurant in Indiana. Frank and Dan pounced on him. All they knew about the taste of pizza came from the magazine's description. And they had never met anyone who had baked a pizza. The Carneys offered Bender a partnership in their budding venture and he accepted.

The mother supplied the capital, $600 borrowed on a paid-up insurance policy. The whole operation fell together. Expansion never stopped. In 1977, Pepsico paid $7 million for the Pizza Hut system, and Frank stayed on as president. Dan, an addicted entrepreneur, left to open another business, including some Pizza Hut franchises among his assets.

But a lot of happenstance was involved here. The brothers had several intangibles working for them. First, the family was in the food business. The new entrepreneurs could buy materials at a good price through the store. And, because the Pizza Hut was too small, some of the ingredients were prepared in the family grocery store. They lucked into a craze that was just beginning to sweep the country. No one ever did figure out what made pizza so popular at the time. One theory was that American soldiers stationed in Italy brought back a desire for pizza, but the war had been over for more than a decade in 1958. The magazine article was prescient. Most of the pizza parlors in the United States were located on the East and West Coasts, not in the American heartland. Even the franchising was accidental. One of the Carneys' employees, enthusiastic about the potential of pizza, asked for the right to open a similar restaurant in Topeka, Kansas. "We had more guts than brains," Frank admits today.

Colonel Harland Sanders turned business adversity into his world-famed Kentucky Fried Chicken franchise business. He was almost sixty when he learned that plans were under way to move the highway from the doorway of his restaurant in Corbin, Kentucky. Soon the off-ramp that funneled customers into the parking lot was moved. In 1952 Colonel Sanders saw hard times ahead for his restaurant and sold his first KFC franchises. In 1956 the death blow struck, an interstate highway was built seven miles from the restaurant. At age sixty-five, Colonel Sanders was "just about broke." He piled his chicken-frying equipment and samples of his seasoning blend into an old car and visited restaurants, signing franchise contracts with any that recognized the wonders of his special-recipe fried chicken. "We couldn't have lived without that $105 a month Social Security check," he recalls. KFC grew fast and profitably and was acquired by Heublein in 1971. Colonel Sanders, almost ninety years old, still is very much in the act as goodwill ambassador for the chicken that made him famous and rescued him from poverty.

Bookkeeping

In studies detailing the problems that beset small businesses, faulty bookkeeping comes high on the roster of culprits. Records are not kept, or kept ineptly. Some small-business owners are incapable of keeping their books up to date or fail to recognize how to use the financial information that good books give to correct operational errors. For the business newcomer, a bookkeeper or certified public accountant is a worthy investment, unless your business is small and you are familiar with a workable bookkeeping system. As long as it works for you, don't worry if it seems amateurish. But when the paper work keeps you away from the stove or the business, you will know it is time to seek professional help. As one business adviser said, "A competent accountant is well worth his fee. He can save you time, headaches, and expenses."

You can locate a good accountant by asking the bank, business friends, or the owner of a small business. Avoid hiring a relative; it can lead to future troubles. You do not need a fancy accounting firm, but it should not be someone with a full-time job elsewhere who is just looking to pick up a little extra money. There are plenty of competent accountants who can be hired by the hour.

But do not stop there. Go over the books now and then. Even a layman can tell if receipts, bills, canceled checks, and the like are being processed properly. An accountant's performance can mean success or failure for a young business. Jeff Perlman, the Party Box partner, recalled, "We went through a number of accountants. They were inefficient and gave us bad advice. The records simply were not kept. Now we have a good one, but it took him three or four years to straighten things out. All the papers, the records, were sitting in boxes and boxes on the floor."

Law and Regulations

The constant lament of the small-business man is that the government (with a capital G and pronounced with lots of emphasis), the Government aggravates the difficulties of opening a small enterprise with needless regulations. Suddenly, he is doing paper work for agencies and programs that he might only have been vaguely aware of in the past, such as OSHA (Occupational Safety and Health Administration) and affirmative-action programs (to promote the hiring of women and minorities). "All this means a drain on early sales that eats away profits," one small-business man groused.

To lead you through this governmental maze, you need a lawyer. Not necessarily a high-powered attorney from the community's leading firm. Just a lawyer with a good reputation with whom you feel comfortable and in whom you have confidence. Use the same guidelines as in the selection of a bookkeeper. Get recommendations from the bank and business friends. The food industry happens to be one of the most closely regulated fields in business, and you will need a competent adviser.

A New York State Department of Commerce booklet explained the reason for the stringent regulations: "The laws covering home production serve two basic purposes. They protect the community through zoning, vending, and labor controls and protect the customer by requiring sanitary production and honest labeling."

One important point: The workroom—in your case, the kitchen—is subject to regulation, and this usually means that it must be devoted exclusively to food production for outside use. In most states, the family kitchen will not do. Regulations are detailed, covering condition of the floor, food-handling equipment, drains, windows, etc.

Many owners of small retail service firms do not consult a lawyer until an emergency arises. By then, the damage might already have been done. This false economy could result in the loss of your business. The NYS Department of Commerce pointed out, "In comparison to the money risked in starting a new business, an attorney's fee is easily justified." The Small Business Administration seconded the view: "The complexity and volume of these laws make it impossible for small marketers . . . to know all of their opportunities and rights and to recognize their liabilities."

Insurance

For a person cooking at home or selling his or her services as a cook, insurance coverage need not be extensive. A good casualty insurance policy will protect you if an employee or part-time helper falls down the stairs or someone claims your food is bad. Madeline Poley, who ran a specialty-food store in New York City, noted, "People think they've been poisoned at the slightest stomachache so we carry full liability insurance." Operators of food stores and restaurants that carry heavy capital investments should be covered for fires and other disasters that could disrupt business and, of course, against the liability for customers and employees. Remember, whether or not the employer is negligent, he or she is considered liable for any injuries on the premises.

Getting Under Way

With these hard facts of business in mind, you are ready to start your own business. For the prospective owners of a restaurant, once the concept of the operation is crystallized, the procedure is clean-cut. Secure the proper financing and credit sources. Find a good location. Line up the suppliers. Buy or lease the equipment.

But for a person trying to sell individualized services or foods, the route is less defined. The entrepreneur must go out and search for markets, in food stores or in less obvious outlets, such as specialty departments in department stores. For both, the opportunity is there. For success you need the proper money, imagination, energy, knowledge, skill, and, yes, luck. We're going to tell you more about all this in the pages that follow.

Chapter 3

The Key to Catering

Until World War II catering in small towns, villages, and many cities in America was monopolized by women eking out meager incomes, oblivious to the realities of business. To be sure, these cateresses decorated impressive wedding cakes, spread millions of pastel finger sandwiches, and made tons of chicken salad. They were regarded as local authorities on fine foods, and a few of them were immortalized in recipes remembered years after their reigns as queens of party-giving. Miss Jennie Benedict's rum cakes are still baked in Louisville, Kentucky, and older folk nostalgically recall her elegant collations. Miss Alberta Patterson in Tallahassee, Florida, is remembered for her wickedly rich coffee frappé.

Catering has come a long way since chicken salad, rum cake, or coffee frappé made a caterer of you. The catering business in cities is dominated by sharp business people. Even in remote areas where able women or men might cater parties as spare-time jobs, competition is ever present in the mobility of the big-time caterers who can truck food and staff from nearby cities. Restaurants, country clubs, and volunteer groups who do parties as fund-raising projects compete with small caterers.

A good head for business and an almost heartless attitude toward demanding a fair price for your services make a caterer of you. If you can make money at it, then let your creative urge run wild, making sure you get paid for every fantasy you and the customer agree upon. The enjoyment of catering is practical only as long as the customers pay, and you keep an eye on the balance sheet.

Part Time

Even today, a catering business can be operated part time, and almost all caterers have seasonal slumps and rushes. A young advertising woman in New York City caters small wedding and cocktail parties near her family home in Southampton on weekends. A schoolteacher in Georgia caters during her Christmas vacation and two months in the summer. A restaurant cashier in Miami makes extra Christmas money by creating and selling frozen hors d'oeuvre to hostesses who will pay a premium price for handmade, super-quality food. A chef's wife and mother of two school-age daughters in Traverse City, Michigan, caters from September until late July, when the family vacations on their houseboat moored in Lake Michigan.

A part-time catering business operated from home requires less capitalization than full-time catering from a commercial kitchen or commissary, but there still is a capital outlay to start. It is illegal in most localities to cook food for sale in your own kitchen. Catering is rigidly controlled by health departments due to the dangers in food prepared in one location, transported and served in another location, sometimes from a buffet or kitchen with inadequate heating and refrigeration facilities.

Anne Steeg had a separate kitchen built in the basement of her home in Traverse City, using family savings as her capital. The kitchen has a drain in the floor, required for easy cleaning, and equipment required by the health code. She purchased used refrigerators, ranges, and other large equipment from a restaurant in Urbana, Illinois, that was going out of business. This included a meat slicer, grinder, and heavy-duty mixer, which she considers essential for whipping up cheese and other spreads.

Mrs. Steeg uses the family station wagon for deliveries. Her menus include hot and cold hors d'oeuvre, so she purchased racks holding sheet pans (available from catering supply houses) and packs them in huge coolers in the station wagon. Hot-food carriers are covered with insulating wrappings to keep the foods at the required 145 degrees for safety.

Chafing dishes with water baths and heaters help keep foods at safe temperatures on the tables, and these cost about $150 each. Mrs. Steeg sometimes works in locations with no heating and refrigeration facilities, so her transportation and heat-holding equipment are essential for keeping foods fresh tasting, as well as safe for serving. How she handles her menus, labor supply, and other facets of her business are detailed further throughout this chapter.

Gladys Clark, a second-grade teacher in Atlanta, is catering part time as an investment in her future, planning to go full time when she retires from teaching. Meanwhile, she works from her home kitchen, and in the ten years she has been in business has been able to purchase silver candelabra, silver punch bowls, and trays that are the mark of her parties. She has had tablecloths made in several pastel shades and white satin, so a hostess can choose a color scheme for a party, and Mrs. Clark supplies napkins to match. Profits from the business also have gone into the large heavy-duty cookware needed for catering. She transports foods in ice chests in her automobile and uses the hostess's refrigerator to keep foods at safe serving temperature after she arrives at the home.

Mrs. Clark has escaped any business reverses that required a loan or other emergency financial help, but has made little money. She thinks her profits show in the equipment she has accumulated to set her up in full-time business with a minimum of investment capital a few years from now. Later in this chapter, we will tell you how Mrs. Clark and her crew handle their parties.

Full Time

Samuel A. Milliken could not even cook when he was virtually thrust into a catering business, A Private Town-house Affair, in New York City in the early 1970s. He had leased a townhouse, the former Bulgarian embassy, as a teachers' center for workshops and seminars. Teachers' use of the center declined almost before his project was started due to budget cutbacks in the school system. Casting about for ideas to bring in money, he first rented a cardroom to a bridge club, then occasionally to other groups for parties. He subcontracted food at first. About 1971, he hired a cook and planned cocktail buffets and sit-down meals.

"I found I liked to cook, and did some things very well," he says. Now he is so busy with sales, paper work, and distribution, he almost never cooks except to show a new helper how to prepare a dish. Where it is germane to the subject, Sam's operation is discussed throughout this chapter.

Jane Wilson had worked for ten years as an ad copy-writer on foods for an agency in New York City. She was familiar with recipe development and food presentations for advertisements. But she wanted something more, a chance to do something innovative with foods, she thought. She quit her job, took several cooking and food-service management courses, and opened her catering firm, the Party Box. From 1967 to 1969 she worked out of her apartment kitchen, with a freezer purchased for the business in her bedroom. She poured more money into the business, $8,000 from personal savings, when she moved to a storefront kitchen and retail shop in 1969. She sold desserts and other items retail.

Sally B. Robinson, a divorced mother of five, commuted to her job in New York City from her home in Rocky Hill, New Jersey. She read a local newspaper, even the want ads, on the train. The numerous ads for cooks to prepare dinner struck her eye, and Sally herself often yearned for a good meal ready to serve when she dragged home after a hard day as an administrative assistant in a hospital. She lost her job in a budget cutback at the hospital in 1977. With no income and no job opportunity in sight and five children to support, she remembered the ads for cooks for dinner. She started Sally's Supper Service, home-delivered dinners for working wives or anybody who wanted a hot meal. Almost a year and a half later, she delivers ten to fifteen dinners an evening. If nobody is at home and she is told where to find the key, she will put the dinners in the oven and turn it to low, to keep dinner hot until the family arrives home from work and school. Sally has taken larger parties, and at this writing was pondering development of her business to include more large parties. Her largest party to date had a hundred and fifty guests, a wedding reception a week after Christmas. There were so many mishaps on that occasion that she described it as a "Lucy Show," but luckily the chaos was behind the scenes, not apparent to the hostess and guests, who seemed pleased with her service.

Ms. Robinson describes the day. She arose at 3:30 A.M. to start cooking. The health inspector had warned her sternly of the danger of cooking too much food ahead since she had only one family-size refrigerator. She heeded his advice carefully. All tasks and a proposed time schedule were written on a large blackboard so she and her helpers—two neighbors, one daughter, and two tall sons—knew what was to be done.

Sally Robinson first made the miniature quiche shells—four or five hundred of them. About 5:30 A.M. she was baking the last batch or two when she noticed that the oven cut off periodically. The awful truth dawned on her —the tank of propane gas that fueled her oven was running low. She still had tiny cream puffs and fifteen turkey breasts to bake. Instead of panicking, she phoned the answering service of the gas-tank delivery service and was assured the truck would be dispatched as soon as the first driver came to work.

Meanwhile, her crew of helpers gathered and she asked the next-door neighbor, who was engaged as a helper, to bake the several hundred cream puffs. "We started everything we could properly do without an oven, which really wasn't much."

To compound the problems, the refrigerator, loaded with jellied salad molds, was powered by the gas, too. "I took the salads out, covered them with plastic, and buried them in the snow," she said. The weather was with her, twenty degrees outdoors and a refrigerator chill in the garage, so she wrapped and kept perishables cold there.

The truck with the propane tank did not arrive until about 2:30 P.M., when Ms. Robinson was almost ready to beg and borrow any available oven in the neighborhood to roast turkey breasts. Then midway in the afternoon the local health inspector, whom Ms. Robinson had made a firm friend of months earlier, phoned to announce a routine inspection.

"That sent us all into a tizzy," she recalls. "It wasn't that we were doing anything illegal, but five people in my small home kitchen! It was a wild scene. I just couldn't have the inspector. I told him to come tomorrow!"

The salads, after their nesting in the cold snow, turned out on their silver platters more beautifully than ever before. Every cream puff, miniature quiche, and every slice of bread was buttered in time for the reception at eight o'clock. The hostess and guests saw a sumptuous buffet, served their plates, and were seated at tables, every detail apparently running smoothly.

But what went on in the background was something else! Having a good neighbor is essential. "Without her, I would never have lived through that day," says Sally Robinson, her voice still shaky almost a year later.

Ms. Robinson thinks that working well with people is the most important quality a caterer can have. "That day the esprit de corps was marvelous, something I covet," she says. "We enjoyed the common effort, we all had fun, and I can assure you that by three o'clock that afternoon we were exhausted." The most valuable person on the team is somebody to run errands—her son on that busy, cold day. "You think you've planned everything, but you always forget something."

Jane Wilson and her partner, Jeff Perlman, who came into the business in 1972, and Sam Milliken depend on their businesses for support, and Sally Robinson cannot allow her business to lose money, so none of them can afford to lose money or let cash flow slow down without planning how to tide themselves over slow seasons.

Ms. Wilson works from the fifteen-by-thirty-foot kitchen she moved to in 1969, but has expanded the office space to a building around the corner. Milliken works in a preparation kitchen next to his office, in one of the townhouses where he puts on parties. He uses several townhouses, mostly occupied as offices by organizations, and will cater parties in the customers' locations. If off the premises, he and his staff prepare some food in the prep kitchen and finish it at the party location. Ms. Robinson cooks where she always has—in her thirteen-by-nine-foot honey pine-paneled kitchen, with a tiny pantry for storage and the home-size refrigerator–freezer she had used for her family for several years before.

Menus, Services

Menus are as varied as the caterers and as their customers' wish. Mrs. Clark serves traditional wedding-reception food—a beautiful wedding cake that she bakes and decorates herself, fruit punch and coffee, cheese straws, mints, and tea sandwiches. She does not handle alcoholic beverages, since she has no license, but will put the hostess in touch with a bartender, and the bartender will assist the hostess in purchasing champagne or liquor in the proper amounts. "The food has to taste good, too," Mrs. Clark said. She changes menus from time to time, too, and is always looking for new ideas in the sandwich fillings or tidbits to serve with punch and coffee.

Mrs. Steeg serves hot and cold hors d'oeuvre. Her cold trays usually include at least one impressive meat platter, turkey, ham, or beef roasted in her catering kitchen and arranged and garnished on a tray. Her hot hors d'oeuvre include a Korean-style marinated beef, marinated chicken, hot crabmeat dip with melba toast, and, sometimes, curried seafood or chicken à la king in tiny patty shells. She does not handle liquor and usually serves buffet, so provides no waiters or waitresses. She stays through a party to make sure trays are replenished. For a big party, her husband, a chef, may help replenish trays.

Sally Robinson's dinners sound like what mama cooks, stuffed peppers one night, pork chops and scalloped potatoes the next, and stuffed Cornish hens the following night. She prints menus for a month. A customer may order dinner for one night, one night a week, one week, or for the entire month.

Jane Wilson serves some of the most stylish food in New York. She and Jeff Perlman emphasize display—lavish arrangements of polished fresh vegetables as a decoration, and the salad and food trays as part of the buffet decor. A summer cocktail buffet might include a standing ham with the Party Box's special mustard sauce, a Camembert or caviar brioche, steak tartare, mousse of trout, and a green and white Greek antipasto. Another season the antipasto might be Italian with the colors of Italian sausages set off by tomatoes and peppers. In the winter, a cocktail buffet may include a hot item such as conch fritters, made by a woman Ms. Wilson brings into the kitchen, or Ms. Wilson's own Monterey Jack cheese and chili dip. The Party Box caters twelve months a year, but January, February, July, and August are slow. During these months, Ms. Wilson and Perlman test new recipes, paint the kitchen and office space, have other maintenance work done, and take inventory of stocks.

Milliken can provide almost any food a customer wants. He is a constant reader of cookbooks and magazines, clips recipes, and works them into the menu when a customer comes to him for ideas.

A caterer in a southern city specializes in carving-board parties—a standing roast of ham, beef, or turkey on a handsome board, carved at the buffet table, with assorted breads, mustards, mayonnaise, and butter on the side, and such simple accompaniments as a tossed, potato, or bean salad or crudités. In Texas several caterers specialize in barbecue—brisket or other meats grilled and served with a spicy sauce, beans and coleslaw, or tossed greens. A typical Texas dessert, catered party or at home, is fresh Stonewall County peach ice cream or pecan tarts. In Los Angeles several caterers specialize in Cal-Mex foods—enchiladas, tamales, tacos, chili beans, and guacamole. Mexican-style food was a fad with the movie colony for many years, though a more elaborate buffet table with galantines of capon, seafood, mousses, and watermelon baskets might be arranged at another end of the room or patio. Several years ago one catering service provided a vendor's pushcart serving steaming hot dogs and trimmings for poolside parties. Another California fad was Chinese or Japanese cooks, who prepared sukiyaki or Teppan steak over a grill set up in the patio.

One hostess on Long Island requested a Sunday afternoon wedding reception menu of several kinds of pâté. The caterer fulfilled the request, adding thinly sliced firm breads and cornichons, the tiny sour pickles usually served with pâté, and relishes to cut the richness of the pâtés. Champagne was poured with the pâtés and the wedding cake, cut and served with a sherbet mold later.

The traditional sandwiches, chicken salad, and punch still are requested by some customers, and most caterers can create such a menu to order. But the gourmet fever has hit catering, too. A caterer who hopes to grow must change menus as consumer tastes change. Fifteen years ago few people had heard of quiche, much less expected to have it served at a cocktail buffet. Today it is almost a cliché. And to people like Jane Wilson, the something new, the chance for creativity, keeps the challenge of the business alive.

Menus of previous successful parties make a convenient selling tool for a caterer when interviewing prospective clients. This menu for dinner for five hundred and fifty guests and late supper for three hundred, a benefit party on a hospital ship, is one of Jane Wilson and Jeff Perlman's show-off examples of an elaborate party.

MENU

DINNER FOR FIVE HUNDRED AND FIFTY:

Hors d'oeuvre:

Baskets of crudités—Sauce niçoise
Caviar brioche
Steak tartare on pumpernickel
PuPus
Seviche en brochette

Dinner:

Gazpacho
Rare filet mignon in vol au vent
Sauce béarnaise
Mousse of trout
Salad of endive, watercress, and
mushrooms

Dessert:

Zabaglione and strawberries
Coffee

LATE SUPPER FOR THREE HUNDRED:

Blini with sour cream and
smoked salmon
Green grapes

The service from each caterer varies, too. Ms. Wilson and Perlman arrive with everything—from the first bite of food to the last napkin to wipe the guests' fingers. The Party Box provides waiters, waitresses, Ms. Wilson or Perlman to supervise, and a pack-up crew to clear the kitchen afterward.

Gladys Clark brings the serving crew, but for a small party this may be only two or three people. Mrs. Steeg, as noted, works a party alone, serving buffet style, with the host or hostess responsible for any help to empty ashtrays or mop up accidental spills. Ms. Robinson uses help for a large party, in the kitchen and party rooms, but has no help with dinners.

Sam Milliken provides everything—waiters, waitresses, cooks, a supervisor, every chafing dish, tray, the liquor, wine, flowers, and, if requested, the music.

Labor Pool

Mrs. Steeg obviously has the easiest labor supply—herself and the occasional help of her husband, a professional chef. So far, illness or a personal emergency has not kept her off the job.

Ms. Wilson and Sam Milliken use the vast resource of part-time workers in New York City—actors and actresses between jobs. The caterers pay $4 to $5 an hour. Ms. Wilson also uses students, and her preparation kitchen on Columbus Avenue is handy to hundreds of young folk looking for part-time and spare-time jobs. Some cooks work with her a few hours a week, specializing in one food, such as the mustard sauce. She insists that celery be cut on a certain slant for a look she wants. A part-timer may mutter testily at first that "she is so fussy." But when "we get it put together and he sees how great it looks, he's an expert at the job from then on," she said.

Ms. Wilson bubbles enthusiastically by nature and shows excitement openly when a food looks and tastes

beautiful. The enthusiasm is contagious. On-the-job training takes a lot of her time and patience, but is worth it
for the effect she wants in her parties.

The Party Box also has two full-time staff members, in
addition to the partners, an office manager who handles
phone calls and pre-selling, and a kitchen manager.

Milliken has become so deeply involved in arranging
parties in his spaces—which now include a loft as well as
the several townhouses—sales, paper work, and supervision that he has hired chefs and assistants. He may do
as many as three parties a day, so obviously he cannot
cover all locations.

In addition to between-engagement actors, Ms. Wilson
discovered an Irish family soon after she started business.
They carried the word to friends and friends of friends,
so many of her waitresses come from a small Irish colony
in the Bronx.

Mrs. Clark's labor pool is built-in—her parents and children. "It is too hard to keep other people employed since
I work spasmodically," she said, "and the really good people want regular jobs."

When Ms. Robinson has a large party she hires friends
and neighbors in Rocky Hill to help her. This has worked
out so far, but if she increases her large-party business,
she realizes she must develop a larger labor pool.

Equipment

Serving pieces, linens, tableware, even tables and chairs
can be rented in almost any city. Some caterers find
rentals more economical than providing storage space for
large numbers of tables. Many caterers also use disposable
dinnerware and barware, which offers an advantage in
sanitation as well as cost of breakage and cleanup time.

Ms. Robinson uses about half disposable materials in

packing dinners. When she does a party, she uses her own silverware and linens or borrows from neighbors. She borrows cookware from a neighbor, too.

Mrs. Clark has purchased her table serving pieces a few at a time, so now is equipped to do a party for one or two hundred guests. Milliken also has bought his dinnerware, glassware, linens, tables, and chairs bit by bit until he can handle a party for four hundred and fifty with no renting, though he rents tables and chairs occasionally.

Mrs. Steeg purchased her equipment, but uses some disposable dinnerware. The Party Box owns most of its accessories, silverware, tableware, barware, and linens.

Women and men who start out catering little dinners for six to twelve often rely on their own dinnerware to set tables. Renting equipment is almost as expensive as owning it, Milliken points out, and you have to return it washed, though not necessarily sanitized.

Setting Your Prices

Most caterers charge a certain price per guest, the cost computed on the price of the food plus labor and overhead. Ms. Wilson charges $8 to $10 per person for a cocktail buffet. She figures this as about 60 percent markup over the cost of the food. That allows for the cost of labor, transportation, and overhead. She cautions that buying wholesale is not necessarily a savings. She buys canned goods in wholesale-size cans, but meat, produce, and almost everything else cost more than at the neighborhood supermarket. She uses a service market for produce, as well as specialty-produce merchants. She gets the high quality essential to mammoth vegetable displays and taste standards but pays a premium for it. She shops at a specialty meat market, paying extra for reliable quality.

Ms. Wilson says her markup is modest by New York

standards, since many caterers get an 80 percent markup over cost of food. "I feel I create volume for my kind of service with these prices," she said, "and I have some corporate customers that spend $20,000 a year with me."

At the other end of the price range is Mrs. Clark in Atlanta. Her charge will be $2.00 to $2.50 per guest. Her menu is much simpler than that of the Party Box, but almost never includes meat except in a sandwich spread, and she has neither the full-time staff nor the rental and other overhead that Ms. Wilson and her partner have. Mrs. Clark also rarely does a party for more than one or two hundred guests, so does not have to be set up for huge events.

Milliken charges $25 to $45 per person for major functions—cocktail buffets including hot and cold foods or sit-down dinners. The price of good food is about the same for any menu, he figures, so his charges are based on the length of the party, the staffing, and the number of guests. The shorter cocktail reception will require less food and a smaller payroll than a sit-down dinner that will go for three or four hours.

Ms. Robinson set a price at first of $6 for two dinners delivered to the same house, but soon realized she was making only a meager profit. She now charges $8 for two dinners, $10 for three, and $12 for four. The menu is set, so she can calculate the cost four or five weeks in advance, barring unexpected price changes at the supermarket, where she shops.

Working with Customers

The first interview with a prospective bride's mother can be a disastrous or a warm experience. Both Anne Steeg and Jane Wilson prefer corporate customers, because business persons managing such work negotiate in a businesslike manner and corporate business returns year after year in many cases. The private-party hostess often is a onetime customer, for a bar mitzvah or the wedding of her only daughter. She often is unaware of the costs a caterer must cover—insurance, overhead, transportation, the added cost of party-quality food, and payroll. She is shocked that fruit punch will be $1.50 or $2.00 a gallon when she can make it for 65 cents a gallon, easily, she thinks, and she never heard of corkage, the cost of having a waiter or waitress open the wine she buys.

Mrs. Clark prefers the private customer. They're instant pay, a deposit of half the estimated cost when the contract for the party is signed and the remainder the day of the party. Companies may pay bills only once a month, and if your bill arrives the day after, it may be two months before you are paid. Ms. Wilson plans for such conditions, after having had some frustrating years of waiting for slow payment while her taxes and rent came due. Mrs. Clark phones a few days before the party to get a final count on guests, ask if there are any minor changes in menu—and to remind the hostess that the final check is due when Mrs. Clark arrives with the food, waiters, and waitresses.

Milliken accepts private, group, and corporate parties. However, he gives a hostess shopping around a rule-of-thumb price on the first telephone contact. If his price is too high, time won't be wasted in futile negotiating.

Milliken schedules parties three to four months in advance, and for special dates, weddings, bar mitzvahs, or anniversaries, as much as a year in advance. However, he will work a party on two or three weeks' notice if the time is open.

Mrs. Clark works weeks or months in advance on her schedule. Mrs. Steeg works in a small city, so often can handle a party on a few weeks' notice. She prefers parties she can put on her calendar months in advance. One trade-association customer has a party every January, so as soon as the date is set, she begins to plan for it.

Ms. Robinson can take dinner orders a day or two before delivery, but she books larger parties several weeks in advance.

How to Get Customers

Jane Wilson's parties have been mentioned in *The New York Times*, national magazines, *Women's Wear Daily*, and almost every important media outlet in New York City. It took her until 1972 to make $30,000 gross sales. But she also had $12,000 loans outstanding and took in her partner with a $5,000 investment. She is now at about $250,000 gross sales annually, making a profit, and has paid herself a salary all along.

With the help of an accountant costing out her operations, she realized the retail business was unprofitable, due to the heavy inventory she had to carry. As a result, she went more heavily into wholesale, selling desserts to gourmet food shops and soups, salads, and other foods to the café at the Guggenheim Museum. Now, since she has developed several solid corporate accounts, Time, Inc., among them, she has dropped the dessert sales. Charity parties are a solid source of income as well as publicity, and she still does a few weddings and bar mitzvahs. The reputation of the Party Box for innovative, beautifully designed parties has blossomed, and after several worrisome years Ms. Wilson and Perlman still work hard but now can count their profits, plan for the slow months and the slow pay of some corporate customers.

Sam Milliken's townhouse parties achieved a status through word of mouth when he put a single ad in *New York* magazine—"Have your party in my fine townhouse."

The first ad brought phone calls by the dozens and he has run ads every week since in *New York,* now advertises in *The New York Times* and other media. He can hardly handle all the business that comes his way for parties in townhouses, clubs, a loft he uses, and in clients' homes.

Gladys Clark's business has been promoted through the grapevine, starting with a cake she did for a sister-in-law's wedding, and from there her business grew so that now she turns down more customers than she accepts.

Ms. Robinson took an ad in her local newspaper when she started her dinner-on-wheels service and has run it regularly ever since. One customer telling a friend brings her business, too.

Rewards

Sam Milliken's days of school teaching are far behind him, and though competitors have set up party businesses in townhouses, he says, "It's not bad for me at all. Theirs introduces the idea of mine, too." The idea works in Hollywood—where one mansion, formerly a center of movie colony shindigs, now can be rented for parties—and also in some other cities.

Jane Wilson has fulfilled a creative urge to set food styles. Her works are known nationwide, and a party that turns out beautifully gives her the thrill of showing off her culinary artistry.

Anne Steeg "enjoys every bit of it." She worked in a gift shop until she realized her real interest was in serving delicious food in a pretty setting.

To Gladys Clark, her business is "like therapy." She forgets the workaday worries and frustrations of teaching when she is fussing with dainty sandwiches and decorating a cake. She revels in the party itself. "I feel almost like the mother of the bride." When she does a reception for one bride, if there is a younger sister, she starts talking up that reception a few years hence.

Sally Robinson's big moment was a woman saying to her: "Are you the famous Sally Robinson?" She thinks the woman was referring to her "guts to do it, not that I did anything all that right!"

Catering takes guts. A party can be like opening night at the theater—nervous moments, stage fright among the helpers, the forgotten Sterno. Experienced hands such as Jane Wilson, Sam Milliken, Anne Steeg, Gladys Clark, and Sally Robinson learn how to deal with disasters calmly and efficiently. A caterer becomes a style-setter in cuisine in his or her locality, too—like the famous Sally Robinson.

It took Jane Wilson almost ten years to adapt her business system and psyche to slow-paying customers. It took ruthless cutting back in her retail sales and other low-profit items.

Now she is confident that she can stick with the fantasy that made her leave a secure job for the insecurity of going it alone as a caterer, a dream that she could be involved in producing fine and beautiful food. She and her partner, Jeff Perlman, love every backbreaking chore of creating the gastronomic still-lifes that the Party Box is known for in New York City.

Every caterer we interviewed feels a swell of pride in a party to stun the eyes and tastes of the guests. A few we interviewed are no longer working. The drudgery was too much for them. One woman in Idaho still is trying her wings at catering. She's learning fast to quote a price and stick with it—after a customer insisted on a buffet for a hundred and fifty guests for $200. It was impossible! Now this caterer has had printed a set of menus at different prices per guest. She still is free to make a minor substitution if she has a new dish or if the hostess has a recipe she wants duplicated.

But catering hardly qualifies as a business if it doesn't pay you for your time, as the caterer in Idaho is just learning, and Jane Wilson and Sam Milliken, who live by their catering, know. It isn't sufficient just to feast their egos on the quality jobs they do.

Chapter 4

Making a Business Out of Your Specialty Dish

In 1978 the fastest-selling line in dozens of specialty-food shops around the country was Judy and Toby's jalapeño jellies. Less than four years earlier the two women were bribing Toby's teenage son to unload cartons of precious jelly glasses in which to pack the next batch of jelly.

Judy Simon and Toby Wank ineptly started their business the summer of the canning-jar shortage. While home canners were going crazy hunting preserving jars and lids, Judy and Toby feared their fledgling business would die in the nest until they talked a supplier into allotting them a few cases of jelly jars with lids.

To go back to the early 1970s, Judy and Toby, friends and neighbors in Woodland Hills, California, a suburb of Los Angeles, were catering frozen hors d'oeuvre and desserts, so named their business Beginnings, Endings, Etcetera. They did the cooking and had occasional child- and husband-labor help for deliveries and picking up supplies. Would it not be simpler, they asked themselves, to narrow down and concentrate on the jalapeño jelly they spread with cream cheese on canapés? Everyone went out of the way to comment on it. They sealed it in jars, so it took no freezer or other special storage. It could be packed in large batches, sixty cases in an eighteen-hour-day for both of them in Toby's kitchen. Jelly-making days were exhausting, but they kept up with orders for several years with two or three days a week in the kitchen.

Their first retail outlet was a fancy foods and gift boutique in Woodland Hills. The jellies sold and sold, so Judy and Toby geared up to expand. Using a family kitchen violated health regulations, and they knew it. Judy had worked at the county health department before she was married. But they never had a mishap, due to taking meticulous precautions and working brutally hard—and maybe lots of luck.

However, after a year and a half in Toby's kitchen, they rented a camp kitchen near their homes, got the proper license and inspection, and continued to turn out jelly in huge batches with almost no help. Eventually, they contracted manufacture of the jellies to a commercial processor who packs to their specifications.

Judy and Toby have become super saleswomen, president and vice-president of Beginnings, Endings, Etcetera, Inc. After their first year they totalled their profits to find out that they had made less than the minimum wage if they counted the hours they put into the business—"But it was better than spending $50 an hour for a shrink, like lots of women we see!" they agree.

Soon business became so brisk that their husbands insisted that they incorporate. Toby's husband, a lawyer, and Judy's, an insurance man, could imagine some terrible accident resulting from a faulty jar of jelly, and the liability falling on their shoulders. Judy and Toby borrowed $100 each from their husbands to incorporate, and paid them back from profits a month later. The profits have gone up steadily ever since, but Toby and Judy reinvest profits in the company, impractical for a person who must make an income out of a business.

Judy and Toby don't recommend starting a food-manufacturing business at home without appropriate licensing and kitchen installation. But cooking at home for sale or producing a good home recipe in a commercial kitchen is almost as old as cooking itself. Sally Lunn gave her name to a rich bread that she peddled and presumably baked at home in Bath, England. The Byrd Cookie Company, started in the 1920s in Savannah, Georgia, baking benne seed wafers by regional recipes, is operated today as a million-dollar-plus business by Benjamin T. (Cookie) Byrd, Jr., the son of the founder. Hundreds of milling companies still operating in this country or absorbed into huge food processing corporations began as family flour or grist mills.

Within the memory of almost any middle-aged American who grew up in a small town are local women who bolstered family incomes by selling homemade breads, cakes, pies, pickles, and preserves and their surplus milk, butter, and eggs. Until recent years, the Germans in southeastern Ohio stored excess milk as homemade cheese in cool cellars and sold it to Sunday drivers from Cleveland and Akron. The Pennsylvania Dutch started family businesses with their homemade sausages, pickles, relishes, and preserves, and sold them in regional markets.

But the demise of the home kitchen as a commercial kitchen has not killed specialty-food manufacture. On the contrary, never have sales been so hot for unusual food items, due in part to the growing number of working women with dwindling time for fancy cooking and the rising income to pay well for unusual foods. Producers are cooking and packing fine family recipes in commercial canneries, creameries, and bakeries for the fame, profits, and fun their own businesses bring.

Ilse Goldberger in Cheltenham, Pennsylvania, served a quiche at a cocktail party in 1965, friends asked her to make quiches for their parties and, in a few months, her husband Irvin was coming home at lunch to help roll out quiche crusts while she mixed fillings and baked quiches for sale. From these home-kitchen beginnings, the Goldbergers' quiches and other specialties have grown to national distribution. We'll tell more about their business development later.

Marie Simmons, who supplies desserts to a restaurant, has built a commercial kitchen in the family brownstone in Brooklyn. Until her death a few years ago, a woman in Cloverdale, California, supported herself and her ailing husband from a kitchen she had built in the lush vegetable and herb garden in the backyard of their home. There she handmade ravioli, froze and sold it to drive-in customers. Family cheese factories are operated in barns on farms in California, Wisconsin, New York State, Oregon, and other parts of the country. Women have built candy kitchens in the basements and in wings added onto their houses or garages remodeled to meet local health standards for commercial kitchens.

Four Questions

Before you stake your life savings on a kitchen, contract with a food processor to produce your cherished recipes, or invest your time and energies in selling a specialty food, browse in the fancy-food shops in nearby cities and anywhere you travel, purchase, and taste any items similar to yours, read fancy-food catalogues, and then ask and answer these questions honestly:

1.   Is your food distinctive enough to compete with similar items? Most important of all, is it superior to or different from anything packed for supermarket sales? A small producer cannot hope to compete with a large manufacturer due to the higher markup necessary to keep a small business financially sound.

2.   Will your food appeal to enough buyers to be profitable? If you want to sell nationally, give careful consideration to regional preferences. Many good regional foods, such as Creole seasonings and Texas chili powder, are in limited national distribution because of lukewarm response to them in other areas.

3.   Can you price your specialty to compete with similar products? A gifted home baker in Miami in the 50s and 60s sold superlative cakes at $12.50 and more, each. But she made only an occasional sale, perhaps two cakes a month. The cakes, rich with ninety score butter, the very finest chocolate, and hazelnuts and the freshest eggs, were worth every penny. But Elsa's cakes were not that much better than those sold by a good local bakery. In the bakery, similar but not quite so good cakes were available for half the price. Elsa went to her grave disgruntled that people didn't appreciate her dedication to an almost impossible ideal. A friend commented sadly after she died, "If only Elsa hadn't insisted on using the egg the minute the hen laid it!"

4.   Can you manufacture, sell, and ship the food with a minimum of problems? Can it be stored in a warehouse or can you lease freezer or refrigerated storage space? Are the principal ingredients easily available or must you schedule production for seasonal supplies? Can you predict price fluctuations of ingredients or will your pricing structure be flexible enough to permit adjustments? Can you package the food attractively and protect the quality in shipment and storage at a reasonable cost? Will it be

expensive to ship or can you sell enough in your area to avoid long-distance shipping problems? Can you get a reliable and competent labor force to assist in manufacture?

If all systems still seem go and you're courageous enough to look ahead to years of hard work, you are now ready to send up a trial balloon.

Draw Up a Game Plan

Presumably, you've tried your jalapeño jelly, quiche, mousse, carrot cake, or whatever you plan to sell, on friends and relatives. Now broaden your test panel. One woman tried her carrot cake at the bake sale at her church. She ran the cake booth, an unexpected burst of generosity to the bazaar committee. But in a long day of selling cakes she heard comments and observed people who bought a slice of cake to sample with tea or lunch, then came back for a half pound to take home. The carrot-cake baker started a small business baking and selling carrot cake at block parties in New York City, a summer weekend diversion that has provided a few extra dollars and satisfying fun.

Or you might test your product as Judy and Toby did, by selling a few jars in a fancy-food shop. Or you might do as Marie Simmons did; send a dozen portions of old-fashioned gingerbread with lemon sauce and chocolate mousse to the restaurant where you plan to sell it, and wait for the results—an order or a refusal. If you don't get an order, ask why and offer to adjust the recipe or the price, if that will stimulate a contract to buy your wares. If you sell desserts to several restaurants, you might alter recipes slightly for each to meet special needs—less spice in the gingerbread at one restaurant, less ham or bacon in a quiche to meet taste preferences and trim the price slightly for another.

Ilse and Irvin Goldberger sold all the quiches they made locally for several months. They were working seven days a week. Irvin, an engineer operating his own firm, decided the frozen-quiche business "was a bigger challenge than what I was doing." With about $300 of family savings, he and Ilse rented a store, installed a small factory, named their quiches Gourmaid, and became full-time food manufacturers. They now have fifteen employees, gross about half a million dollars a year, and ship nationwide—but not without problems. The evening their daughter graduated from high school, a local hotel rush-ordered several hundred cheese pies, so after the graduation ceremony they worked until early the next morning. An ordinary day for the Goldbergers starts about 7 A.M. and ends about 9 or 10 P.M.

"We didn't know what we were doing when we started," says Irvin. "We didn't even have a mixer." But they soon learned. They visited commercial bakeries and saw an eye-boggling array of mixers and other machinery. The Goldbergers now have heavy-duty mixers and lots of other machinery, including the devices designed by Irvin to pressure-shape the rigid plastic containers in which the quiches and cheese pies are packed, frozen, and shipped.

John Slovacek, who operates a sausage-making plant on the family home place in Snook, Texas, made his first batch of sausage, thirty-five pounds, one Saturday night in 1953. He sold every ounce of it the next morning to the few grocery stores in the neighborhood that were open on Sunday. He now has six helpers, makes 650,000 pounds of sausage a year, sells about 90 percent of it wholesale to markets and restaurants within a hundred-mile radius of the plant, and the remainder from a retail shop at the plant.

Starting Your Business

Now that you feel confident that you can sell, see your accountant, lawyer, and insurance man. The foundation of any business—capital to start and keep going until you make a profit, licensing, and setting up an accounting system—applies to the cooking business as well.

Act like you're in business, too. Buyers are reluctant to give you space on shelves if you appear to be a couple of women merely having a fling at jelly making or a man selling a few pounds of sausage until his crop comes in. Buyers want to be assured of supplies when they are ready to reorder. Have professional-looking business cards, catalogue sheets, or price lists printed, and make your bills look professional. Get a business phone and consider using an answering service if you will be away much of the time selling or working with the manufacture of the food. You can't run a business by sharing a phone with a teenager who dashes to answer every ring.

Where, if Not at Home?

The Goldbergers, Slovacek, Judy and Toby (the jelly-makers), and Marie Simmons started at home and survived. In some areas, you can continue to cook at home if your kitchen meets local sanitation specifications or if you build a separate kitchen. John Slovacek's plant is located on the family's home farm, but the plant and retail store are separated from the living quarters. The Goldbergers rented and equipped their first plant away from home and eventually bought a building.

Some small food producers rent space in a food factory and install the necessary food-preparation, cooking, and packaging facilities in the space leased to them. Tomato or fruit canneries in some areas operate seasonally, and the owners often are eager to rent space at off-seasons, if you can adapt your schedule to theirs.

A cooking school in New York City leases the kitchen to a baker who prepares desserts for a neighborhood restaurant. Restaurants sometimes will rent production space at early-morning hours, in a few cases an ideal place to start a pâté-making business or to make prepared and frozen foods that can be frozen and stored in another location. School, camp, and resort kitchens might be available during the months they are closed. In fact, a few resort operators go into the specialty-food or mail-order-food business to make use of their facilities at slack seasons.

If you must set up a commercial kitchen, first consult a real estate agent in your area. He or she may list kitchens with basic storage or cooking facilities already installed. Otherwise, you must install food-preparation, cooking, packaging, and storage equipment, which can be quite expensive. If you rent a small warehouse-type building or a store-type building, make sure it is zoned for manufacture.

A plant near the supply of a major ingredient, for example, near peach orchards if your product will be peach pickles, may be practical. It is less expensive to drive yourself to a factory a few miles away than to have bushels of peaches trucked eight or ten miles from orchards to a plant a few blocks from your home. Zoning may be somewhat less restricted for manufacturing and rentals less expensive outside of town, too.

To find a contract processor to pack a specialty food, ask fancy-food-shop operators, especially any who are

selling your homemade foods, for references to processors
in the area. One canner may pack a dozen or two fancy-
food items on contract and a shop operator will have some
knowledge of the company's ability to meet production
schedules and specifications. Also check the processors
listed in the yellow pages of the telephone directory. There
are listings under Preserves, Jams and Jellies, Candy and
Confections (Wholesale and Manufacturers), and Bakeries and Canneries in most manufacturing areas and many
agricultural areas. Discuss your product and prices in detail with the contract salesperson in companies you consider. If possible, have the company run a sample test.
The contract processor prepares and packs the food to
your specifications (recipe and package design) and will
ship it for you if you contract for this service and you pay
the contract price. Comparison shop for price, service,
and quality.

Packaging

Beauty is more than skin deep in a really good fancy-food
item, but the package sells it. A Scotswoman conceived
the idea of naming gift marmalades and preserves for Mrs.
Bridges, the competent cook in the *Upstairs, Downstairs*
television series. The package designer capped ordinary
preserving jars with paper doilies held in place by rubber
bands, and the Mrs. Bridges items were center shelf, eye
level, the most wanted space on the shelf, in many fancy-
food shops the year of their introduction.

You may visualize your cookies in silver paper cuplets,
your fruitcake centered on a gilt paper doily with a bow
of red ribbon perched atop it, your pickle jar swathed in
bright calico, or your macaroons piled artfully in a gilt
cardboard basket. First, find out if the food will travel in

its fancy dress. Will your wrapping meet local, state, and federal regulations? Federal Food and Drug regulations mandate that certain wrapping materials cannot be used next to food due to the danger of contamination. Will the wrapping keep your food fresh for its estimated shelf life and storage life at home?

Fancy packages must be protected by corrugated cardboard or other cartons for shipping. A gilt paper doily will hardly hold a cake steady for a drive across town, and certainly not for shipping in a cross-country truck with a dozen other cakes, but a carton might be constructed around the fancy gift pack. All bottled or jarred foods must be packed in cartons with separators to prevent breakage. Crocks for cheeses must be sealed tightly to prevent breaking or contamination caused by loose covers. The Basloe family at the Original Herkimer County Cheese Company in New York was asked to test handcrafted crocks. "They were beautiful, but the lids were loose, so didn't hold the cheese spread," said Norma Basloe.

Is the packaging you visualize economically sound? Fancy-food packages can be incredibly expensive. Find out how much your proposed swatch of calico will cost and, more important, how much it will cost to wrap around the jar. Can it be applied by machinery? Ordinary labels can be. Hand-wrapping packages is prohibitively expensive for large-volume packing. To keep your price competitive, calico print labels might be more workable.

The telephone directories of every city and some small towns list numerous package designers. A package designer can refer you to a label designer if his service does not include label design.

Before having labels printed, verify what information is required on them. Some foods, such as jellies, require no listing of ingredients if the product is made according to federal standards. Other foods require an ingredients list. Your state agriculture department can provide you with information on labeling requirements within your state, and the local office of the Food and Drug Administration, usually in the capital city or largest city of a state, can provide you with federal labeling requirements.

Have large quantities of labels printed, which is less expensive ultimately, but don't go overboard. Label regulations change periodically. Producers usually are allowed several months to exhaust supplies on hand, but a small producer may not be able to use several thousands of labels before new regulations become effective.

Packaging for sales to restaurants is less critical, except that the package must hold a cake steady, protect a quiche or crêpes from damage in transit, and keep soup or salad in fresh eating condition until the food is served. Simply printed cartons may be used.

Marie Simmons does her own delivery. She transports cakes and some cake layers in the pans. Having extra pans in her kitchen, she picks up used pans the following day for subsequent bakings. She uses commercial cake cartons and crushes Saran Wrap or waxed paper around the base of a cake to prevent slipping and sliding. A cake in a pan or on a paper liner can be anchored with a thick dab of child's play clay, too. She delivers gingerbread in a baking pan with jars of lemon sauce on the side and typewritten instructions on how to reheat the gingerbread and sauce for serving. As new packaging materials for use in microwave ovens are introduced, fancy-food manufacturers supplying restaurants should investigate the needs of these customers to find if they want or need wrappings that can serve as reheating containers for soups, prepared entrees, or hot desserts.

How to Sell

Marie Simmons had sold her desserts before she left a full-time job to go into business. She had prepared samples, and the partners at Gage and Tollner had tasted them. Her husband, John Simmons, is one of the partners in the restaurant, so her sales were virtually guaranteed. But she still believes strongly in providing a taste.

In New York City competition in desserts and other prepared foods sold to restaurants is fierce. Gage and Tollner serves homemade-type desserts as a promotional feature, so Mrs. Simmons has not been asked to lower her prices to meet competition. Other dessert makers have been forced to meet competitive prices, and as a result they usually had to compromise quality in order to continue making a profit. Part of your selling job may be to convince a restaurateur that quality is worth a premium price.

To sell fancy-food items, if they're really good and unique, is easy once you get started. However, the label introduces a food to new users and is an important sales tool. It should be descriptive and provide suggestions for the use of the product. The label might suggest a fruit jelly as a spread for toast, hot biscuits, or rolls and also as an accompaniment to roast meat, a glaze for ham, or as a dessert sauce, if it is suited to such uses. The label might suggest slicing pound cake and toasting it or tossing cubes of a fruitcake or nutcake with whipped cream for a different dessert. The label on fruitcake should mention wrapping it in foil or a plastic bag and refrigerating it before slicing to help give elegant, thin slices. The label might suggest aging the cake in a brandy soaked cheesecloth.

Judy and Toby advocate show-and-tell for their jellies.

They grab every opportunity to demonstrate their jalapeño jelly. Their first big sale was to a gourmet-food buyer in a supermarket. Months later the buyer was asked what possessed him to make such a lucky buy since the jelly was selling so fast he could hardly keep it in stock. He said, "You can't turn down two good-looking women when one is talking and the other is spreading cream cheese and this spicy jelly so fast you can't get a word in, so you say, 'Yes, I'll buy it.'" Judy and Toby still do demonstrations at food shows and in stores, Judy spreading cream cheese and spicy jelly and Toby extolling its virtues as a condiment with meats or on omelets. They now have a food sales representative. Several, such as the H.G. Norton Company in New Milford, Connecticut, specialize in small fancy-food producers. Judy and Toby go to many fancy-food and gift shows and advertise in fancy-food trade journals.

Food sales representatives are listed in the classified section of the phone directory under Food Products, Manufacturers and Distributors. In a large city the listing may contain hundreds of names, so you're wise to ask a fancy-food-shop owner or gourmet buyer in a supermarket for names of local distributors who specialize in fancy food and small accounts. You will find ads for sales representatives in trade journals published for the fancy-food industry. A distributor charges a small percentage and most show their lines at fancy-food and gift shows, but most importantly, they make sales calls on prospective customers. As you expand, your local distributor can advise on sales representatives in other parts of the country.

The first year or so, Irvin and Ilse Goldberger acted as their own salespersons. They now have sales representatives in all parts of the country. The Gourmaid line now includes nine types of quiches, a cheese pie, and mousses in five flavors. The line is sold in a few supermarkets as well as fancy-food shops and to the restaurant trade.

John Slovacek sticks with "sausage like my father and mother made when we butchered the hogs at home—no newfangled equipment," so confines sales to a hundred-mile radius from the plant. Salesmen in the field represent Slovacek Sausage with wholesale buyers, and John Slovacek, his wife, and members of the family run the small retail shop at the plant.

"I've never tried to expand too much," he said. "When I retire I'll turn the business over to my nephew, and I imagine he'll push sales up into Dallas and get bigger. I've made a good living out of it."

Why Slave over a Hot Stove?

Marie Simmons considers baking old-fashioned gingerbread, carrot cake, and whipping up her sinfully rich chocolate mousse more fulfilling than working in the test kitchen of a large national women's magazine. "I cook what I like to cook," she says.

She also enjoys the freedom of being a homebody—but having a fulfilling job, too. She is at home when her daughter gets home from school, can take her turn in the car pool for gymnastics lessons and other children's activities, and can take a week or two off for a wine- or restaurant-tasting trip with her husband without juggling office vacation schedules.

"I freeze every dessert I can before we leave," she explains, "and Gage and Tollner buys the chocolate mousse and other things that don't freeze well." She has time to take an occasional wine-tasting course in New York, and enjoys a convenience any working woman would appreciate—she is at home when the carpenter, plumber, or electrician arrives, a problem since she and her husband began restoring a nineteenth-century brownstone three or four years ago.

Marie takes no salary, but after three years in business her profits amount to as much as she made in salary in her last full-time job. Her first year in business, she barely broke even. She keeps meticulous books on costs and time, and prices her foods accordingly. A dessert that requires a moderate amount of time is priced at three times the cost of ingredients. One that takes more time, such as a layered raspberry torte, is priced at four times the cost of ingredients. She delivers in the family Volkswagen, but has minimal packaging costs since desserts are served soon after delivery.

Judy Simon and Toby Wank don't take salaries, and due to personal tax situations, and as noted, invest all money possible back into the business. The corporation has been profitable for several years.

John Slovacek went into business for the sole purpose of making an easier living. His story is that he was sitting on a roadside selling watermelons piled on a flatbed wagon one blistering hot day in Texas. "I had farming out of my system by then," he recalls. He wracked his brain for any other way he could support himself. His family, among the earliest Czech settlers in that part of Texas, had made wonderful sausage as long as he could remember. Sausage making seemed a lot easier than sitting in the hot Texas sun to sell watermelons, so he started his sausage business that very night. He has changed his manufacturing methods little since that first try at the sausage business. He expanded the plant once, borrowed $18,000 then, but was able to pay it back within a year or two. In addition to a comfortable living, he feels he has reaped generous rewards in satisfied customers. A man feels pretty satisfied with himself, he says, when a tourist buys $40 worth of sausage, slab bacon, and other things to take back to Dallas.

Irvin Goldberger says, "If you're willing to sacrifice, you will be successful." He and Ilse have had problems, plenty of them—slow pay, weeks when they couldn't pay their own salaries, the price tag on a piece of machinery going up faster than they could raise the money to buy it, and a truckload of quiches thawing before delivery in Florida. But he doesn't pause five seconds when asked if he would do it again. "Yes, we would!" The Goldbergers expect their son to come into the business when he gets his degree in business in a few years.

The one time the Goldbergers needed money badly and couldn't borrow at a bank, Goldberger went to the Montgomery County Industrial Development Commission, which helped find a lender. "Now our credit is so good we could get money on a minute's notice," says Goldberger. "We pay bills almost before we get them."

Cooking as a cottage industry has literally died out, although the State of Maine Development and Agriculture Departments encourage home industry to stimulate the economy in low-employment areas. The Department of Agriculture distributes instructions for setting up home kitchens for commercial baking. A woman in Carthage, Mississippi, still bakes cakes and pies to order. A woman in Montgomery, Alabama, made party mints for sale as a sideline to her full-time job.

The late Margaret Rudkin began baking bread at home to tempt a finicky son, sold it first at Macy's in New York City, then everywhere, to establish Pepperidge Farm. The late Ruth Bigelow and a friend packaged their tea blend and called it Constant Comment, the flagship blend of the Bigelow Company, still operated by Bigelow heirs.

Farmer's markets and women's exchanges also provide outlets for homemade foods in some states. One majestically turbaned woman occasionally sells homemade conch fritters and salad at her stand in the tree-shaded market in Coconut Grove, Florida. Women sell their home-baked cakes and breads at markets in Bethesda, Maryland, and Montgomery, Alabama.

A family in Maine gathers fiddleheads, tender sprouts of ferns, in the pine forests and cans them. They are sold as a delicate vegetable, highly prized by epicures.

Martha and Don Jager in Vinton, Iowa, personally select the popcorn they pack for sale to gourmet shops, unpopped and in novelty mixes.

Your bright idea for a food novelty may be the hottest item in gourmet shops next year—or at least a money-maker and fun for you. Judy Simon and Toby Wank don't care to put in another eighteen-hour day at the jalapeño jelly kettles—but it was fun while they were at it. They still love selling the jellies and overseeing the production —and they're still friends. Not all partnerships turn out so happily, they explain.

A person who likes to cook may think selling his or her secret-recipe pâté or fruitcake is just the job for self-expression. It's fun to prepare your pâté or fruitcake a few dozen times, maybe a few hundred, smelling the marvelous aromas, stealing a taste from the one that crumbled at the edge. But keep in mind that when this is for business the imperfect pâté or fruitcake is a loss of time and labor. And making pâté or fruitcake for profit is not just the nice smells in the kitchen. It is sales, packaging and promoting, and delivering. Your tidy little home-baking business may turn into a frantic search for a processor who can bake to your specifications at a price you can afford. You must set a price that gives you a decent profit and allows you to pay the costs of helpers, packaging, equipment, rent, and the hundreds of other expenses that go into a business.

Chapter 5

A Restaurant, Your Very Own

A restaurant seems glamorous, exciting, and adventurous. It is all these things, but it is also probably the hardest work you will ever tackle. You may work twelve or sixteen backbreaking hours a day, then be faced with a major crisis before you leave for the night. Evaluate yourself on your ability to handle the ups and downs of a business that is risky, too.

"I am tempted to make 'don't' my first piece of advice about starting a restaurant," says Marge Mitchell. Yet she and a partner operated the Bakery Lane Soup Bowl in Vermont for several years, then moved to Prescott, Arizona, where they opened Hopi House, which has made a living for them.

The restaurant business is booming, with more meals being eaten out than ever before. Yet of all restaurants opened, 80 percent fail within five years. Rocco M. Angelo, professor in the school of hotel, food, and travel services, Florida International University in Miami, says, "The smallest ma and pa restaurant requires the same attention to culinary and business detail as the largest, most exclusive restaurant."

Angelo lists as the three major reasons for restaurant failure:

1. Lack of food knowledge.
2. Lack of business knowledge.
3. Insufficient capital while building the business to a profitable level.

Don't go in blind. A person with the magnificent dream should survey the market and competition. Will the kind of restaurant you want to operate draw enough customers to pay its way? Are too many similar restaurants operating in the neighborhood? If you have a shred of doubt, talk to other restaurateurs. Many eagerly share their experiences, even with a potential competitor. Also, bounce your ideas off anybody who'll offer frank opinions, the business people, service station and drugstore operators, barbers and hairdressers in the neighborhood. If there is a chamber of commerce or neighborhood association, their members are an excellent source of opinion on whether your dream of a little restaurant might come true.

Once you have established that your idea for a restaurant is realistic, then look for a building.

Where?

Location, location, location, the late Ellsworth M. Statler, the hotelman, said when asked the most important factor for success of a hotel. Restaurateurs mentioned location over and over as most important to the success of a restaurant. Pinpointing a good location involves studying the competition—current and future—the traffic flow, the numbers and tastes of prospective clientele, and the business climate of the community. Is it blue-collar or professional? Both groups spend heavily eating out—but their tastes differ sharply. Is the neighborhood stable, on the way up or down?

Robert Fredy, seeking a location for his Mimosa Café Française in New York City, had three criteria:

1. He wanted to lease, not buy—a good rule for any new restaurant. Leasing requires less capital.

2. He wanted a space that had been previously used as a restaurant. His limited capital did not allow for major alterations.

3. He wanted a neighborhood that would provide a market for the menu he had in mind, inexpensive French food, crêpes and quiches, for both lunch and dinner business.

A building in the Murray Hill section fulfilled the three requirements—he could lease it at a price he could afford, it had been used as a restaurant so would require few alterations, and the clientele was there. The Mimosa draws lunch business from neighborhood offices and, for dinner, couples from nearby apartment buildings.

Long before he signed the lease, he stood on street corners in a several-block radius at lunch and dinner hours, checking traffic patterns, counting noses, and observing the customers going into the restaurants and coffee shops.

Barbara Witt's research was less formal. As a resident of Georgetown, in Washington, D.C., she had observed the dining-out trends for years before choosing a spot for the Big Cheese. She felt confident that diners in Georgetown would support the international cookery she wanted featured on her menu.

The choice of site may be more emotional than businesslike, and good management can make the restaurant succeed. Marge Mitchell and her partner wanted to move to a warmer climate, so went to Arizona—then they looked for the town. "You may have to try on the town and feel its vibes!" Marge says. Prescott, with a tree-shaded town square, reminded her of Middlebury, Vermont, where the first restaurant she operated had succeeded.

She also cautioned, "Check local liquor and licensing laws, zoning, even how much space is required for parking, and the building safety regulation." She and her partner chose Arizona over New Mexico for Hopi House, since New Mexico's liquor licenses were almost unobtainable and prohibitively expensive. Licenses are issued on the basis of population, a certain number per ten thousand residents.

In choosing an area new to you, check every possible local regulation or complication for doing business. If the building you plan to lease was previously occupied by a restaurant, it probably is zoned for that use, but check any variances that are not transferable, including the liquor license. The bar often provides a restaurant's highest profit margin and can mean the difference between success and failure.

And watch out if a former restaurant space is a bargain! It may be a booby trap—too close to a church or school to get a liquor license, too near neighbors who complain of noise, have poor or inadequate parking space, be hard to get to or be a half block from a rowdy nightclub that discourages restaurant clientele.

It pays to have a lawyer check any zoning and licensing laws. If you want to serve alcoholic beverages, in some states you should look for a lawyer experienced in obtaining liquor licenses before you sign a lease or buy a building.

Some restaurateurs choose their locations because

they're there, and their drawing card is a unique menu or style. People drove miles to Bertha Hinshaw's Chalet Suzanne near Lake Wales, Florida, because of its singular Continental-style menu. The late Mrs. Hinshaw probably defied every rule for restaurant location, design, and most rules for operation, but more than forty years later her son and daughter still run the restaurant successfully in an orange grove in central Florida.

Alyne Stroud opened her café behind her husband's service station on a busy highway in Union Church, Mississippi. Alan and Helen Hooker had moved to Ojai, California, and operated a boardinghouse for vegetarians. The Hookers have long since abandoned a natural-food menu in the Ranch House restaurant that grew out of the boardinghouse, but Alan proudly serves home-baked breads, vegetables, and herbs grown in the Ranch House gardens, as well as meat, fish, and fowl.

Some restaurants are spin-offs from other businesses. The late Elsie and John Masterton became restaurateurs in Goshen, Vermont, out of desperation. They bought a ski resort and never had a good skiing season. They converted their lodge into a restaurant and year-round resort, cultivating a clientele first through advertising in the *Saturday Review* magazine.

Locations in business centers of cities may be too high priced for beginning restaurateurs, though there are exceptions. Look for the developing areas of a city before property values zoom. An intuitive eye for developing neighborhoods, plus help from real estate agents and other business advisers, leads you to such fortunate locations as that found by the owners of the Soho Charcuterie and Restaurant in New York City. Madeline Poley and Francine Scherer, looking for a restaurant location, happened upon a thirty-year-old Italian restaurant site at Spring and Sullivan streets.

The Charcuterie has a distinctive food style and a white-on-white decor that at the time seemed too sophisticated for the neighborhood—but the rent in 1975 was low. Since then, art galleries, other restaurants, and chic nightclubs have opened in the district and the Charcuterie draws customers from fifty blocks and farther uptown.

A new shopping center may offer choice space, but too often is beyond the budget of a beginner, although a shopping center offers certain advantages in parking and customer-drawing benefits. Linda Spasato, who had worked in real estate, deliberately chose a shopping center. After only three weeks of looking, she and her partner, Darlene J. Griffis, leased a shell in a shopping center in Newtown Square, Pennsylvania, in December 1976. Less than two months later they had the necessary equipping and decorating done and opened Café Continentale and the adjoining Cheese Plus, a gourmet shop.

You might be lucky and find an urban area that is being reclaimed. Several daring novices opened restaurants on Union Street, in San Francisco, in the late 1950s and early 60s, when rents were moderate. Union Street has become a fashionable restaurant and boutique section, and some of the pioneers are still there. Columbus Avenue, formerly a dreary-looking street on the West Side of New York City, has become a lively strip of small moderate-priced restaurants.

Restoration areas of central cities offer opportunities to restaurateurs who will take the first chancy steps. Those restoration areas approved for HUD funds offer special financial help to business people, too. Among the redeveloping areas where restaurants have prospered are New Town and Old Town in Chicago, the Oakdale section in Dallas and Morris Avenue, an abandoned warehouse street in Birmingham that is beginning to bloom. Copycat restaurants seem to cluster in restoration areas, however, which can spell failure if you start a duplicate of a restaurant up the street. The first restaurants in Old Town in Chicago tended toward hamburger, health food, and a few ethnic menus. The mix is changing, to offer a better competitive climate, with more ethnic restaurants and a few sophisticated restaurants opening. Matt Deletioglu creates his own competition in New Town, a Middle Eastern restaurant and the French Port, a fresh seafood restaurant, a few blocks away.

Once you've chosen your location, you are ready to plan the use of your space.

Planning Your Space

A cramped kitchen can ruin your dreams of efficient service and any chance of profit in some instances, while cooks stumble over each other. Tables so close that customers can join the conversation at the next table destroy a feeling of peaceful dining, not to mention the efficiency of waiters or waitresses. A restaurant designer can help you decorate the interior and façade to draw customers. A food-facilities designer or engineer can help you lay out your restaurant to avoid traffic jams and impossible physical problems. The fee you pay both may save you money ultimately.

Names of restaurant designers are listed under Food Facilities Consultants in the classified section of the phone directory. Or ask other restaurateurs who designed their space for them and if their layouts work efficiently. Visit kitchens and ask for the names of engineers of kitchens that appear to work well. Manufacturers of kitchen and other restaurant equipment and local utility companies often provide design help for kitchen and service areas or refer you to qualified engineers and interior designers. You will find names of nationally known food-service designers in professional journals, a gold mine of information in this and many other areas of the business for a beginning restaurateur.

If you must rely on yourself, lay out the design, plotting traffic and working space needed. In his book, *How to Plan and Operate a Restaurant*, Peter Dukas recommends that 20 to 40 percent of the total space be allotted to the kitchen and the remainder to the dining room. A few authorities suggest as much as 50 percent of the total space for the back of the house, which includes receiving, storage, food preparation, and cooking.

The dining room includes a service area, where silverware, cups and saucers, extra glassware, and linens are kept. Sugar and cream for coffee, salt and pepper shakers, and serving utensils are kept in the service area.

If you lay out your restaurant, read several of the good restaurant books (see chapter 13) and study sample floor plans carefully. Magazines edited for the restaurant trade publish articles on efficient layouts, often with floor plans. Past issues of many of these magazines are available in large libraries, and the *Readers' Guide* lists articles on layout (and many other subjects) to help you locate literature to meet your needs.

The rules of space allocation may be modified by such factors as menu, speed of service necessary or desirable, and the hours the restaurant is open. You might eliminate soup kettles from your kitchen by purchasing custom-made soups. Salad greens and fruits can be purchased ready to serve, so you may eliminate a preparation sink and table for salads. A few restaurants can operate without kitchens, having mammoth freezers from which commissary-prepared foods are whisked, heated in microwave ovens installed in an area that would qualify as little more than a wide corridor, then turned onto plates for service. However, such a menu has little appeal for the food lover who goes into the restaurant business for the joys of self-expression.

Nevertheless, a dream restaurant menu may have to be adjusted to reality—fewer dishes to be prepared in the kitchen if space is limited, judiciously chosen prepared foods such as desserts or appetizers purchased from suppliers who maintain high quality. You may have to simplify elaborate dining room decor, such as large plants, to make space for more tables.

As a general rule, each customer in a restaurant with cafeteria or simple table service requires fourteen square feet (for the chairs, table, and circulation of waiters or waitresses and busboys), sixteen to eighteen square feet for deluxe service, and twelve square feet for short-order service.

In planning a kitchen, have equipment installed for logical progression from deliveries to storage to food preparation (a sink and chopping boards) to cooking and finally to service. A waiter or waitress should pick up the filled plate and add his or her touches (the sprig of parsley and cup of tartar sauce). To end the meal, the busboy should be able to take dirty dishes to the dishwasher as straight-arrow as possible. Washed dishes should be stored nearby or transferred to carts that take the glassware or dishes to storage places. Unnecessary carrying and cross-traffic result in breakage.

Space is almost never perfect, but good planning can make it more efficient. Barbara Witt of the Big Cheese says, "No matter how well you plan, there never is enough [space]. The major space problem for us is insufficient seating in the dining room for reasonable profit. Otherwise, it is a matter of prodding people [the staff] to use their space efficiently."

The great Antoine's in New Orleans has operated with inadequate kitchen space for more than a century. In

1978 the restaurant management applied for a variance to permit expansion of a receiving area at the rear of the kitchen. With a reputation of fine dining for more than a century, Antoine's can overcome the problems of limited space more easily than a novice in business.

Alterations

Using your space efficiently may require structural changes. Major alterations usually mean dealing with a contractor, obtaining a building permit, and the accompanying building, fire, safety, electrical, and plumbing inspections. The inspections protect you from shoddy or unsafe work, but are a nuisance in delays as you wait for an inspector to okay work before workmen can proceed to the next stage of alterations.

Check local sanitation regulations before you remodel. The building, health, or sanitation department probably will provide this information. Most sanitation codes require easily cleaned flooring, mop boards with smooth surfaces, floor drains, and other specific installations for commercial kitchens. A water heater must supply water hot enough for dishwashing, and the refrigerator and freezer maintain temperatures low enough to keep foods safe, as well as fresh-looking and palatable. Plan how and where you will dispose of garbage. In New York City and other municipalities, a restaurant must hire private firms to pick up garbage, but some cities provide this service to commercial as well as residential buildings. Mechanical garbage disposers can save time and money if local building codes permit them.

Check comfort. Noise, poor air conditioning, odors, and improper lighting can ruin a restaurant's ambiance. If the clatter of silverware resounds, hard surfaces such as windows may need draperies, and walls and ceilings, acoustical coatings. A customer blasted by a draft of icy air or stifled in a hot corner may never come back. Have a competent air-conditioning engineer check for odor exhaust, too. Cooking smells should not be vented into the parking lot.

Check lighting for a pleasant glow, not too bright, but bright enough so the menu can be read and customers won't stumble on steps or against furniture. To give a feeling of security, the parking lot should be well lighted, or arrange for valet parking. In many cities, valet parking is operated as a concession, with the restaurateur getting a percentage.

Buying Equipment and Supplies

Investigate leasing or buying equipment and furniture secondhand. Restaurant-supply houses handle used and, occasionally, rental equipment, as well as new. You also might find used restaurant fixtures and furnishings listed in the classified advertising section of the local newspaper. Secondhand dinnerware can add panache. A restaurateur in North Hollywood, California, proudly used dinner plates carrying the "R" of Romanoff's, the famous Beverly Hills restaurant, after Romanoff closed his establishment and offered the dinnerware to Mme. Panoff at the Moskva Cliff, now retired, too.

In buying supplies, a nearby supermarket may be an adequate source, and some restaurants operate successfully with nothing more. But you will look farther for such ingredients as well-ripened cheese, a year-round supply of high-quality salad greens, and uniform grade in meat, poultry, and fish. Shop around, wholesale and retail, and discuss your menu in detail, the quality you want and the prices with possible suppliers. You may be surprised to find that the extra quality you demand, even if food is purchased in large quantities, is more expensive wholesale than in a supermarket.

Service and credit are factors, too, in the choice of suppliers. Some deliver daily, others less often. Establish credit with suppliers, wholesale or retail, as soon as possible. However, plan to pay cash on delivery for three or four months, since few suppliers will extend credit to a beginner.

Carefully consider cost of prepared food versus food prepared on the premises. An able pastry chef is hard to find, and his space needs are enormous, so it may be economical in salaries and space to purchase pastries and breads. Shop for other menu items that meet your quality standards—soup, salads, pâtés, desserts, and prepared ingredients such as cooked and shelled shrimp and sauce bases. They can save costly time. A full menu of prepackaged foods will have little style and will taste like the fare of dozens of restaurants, but good quiches and a frozen entree or two can expand your menu at a minimum cost and effort.

Developing a Menu

A resort hotel owner in Vermont provided one menu choice each evening—a soup or appetizer such as fresh fruit, a meat such as wine-braised chicken, a good beef stew or her apple-glazed baked ham, vegetables, salad, bread, and desserts. A country town hotel operator in Alabama served a single menu each evening, family-style, heaping platters full with fried chicken, baked country ham, and another meat such as country-fried steak or fried catfish, six or eight vegetables, hot biscuits and cornbread, butter and homemade preserves, and several different cakes and pies for desserts.

Both these dining room operators charged a set price for dinner. They could calculate food costs down to the last penny, the woman in Vermont due to a reservations-only policy, the woman in Alabama due to limited seating with every seat taken every night she opened the dining room.

Developing a menu for a more conventional restaurant is not quite so simple. Barbara Witt in Washington continually tests new recipes. When one is perfected, it is added to the menu and a less popular item usually is dropped. Linda Spasato at the Café Continentale in Newtown Square, Pennsylvania, is so fussy about her spaghetti sauce that almost no cook makes it to please her, so she prepares it herself.

Your motivation to become a restaurateur probably is a dedication to a high taste standard. It is up to you to develop the menu style, test recipes to prevent any mistakes in the kitchen, and prepare the specialties yourself or closely supervise chefs and cooks at work.

Customers eat out for excitement, so dishes on your menu should express the character of your restaurant. Some restaurants build reputations on steak, but it must be the finest steak, maybe higher quality meat than you can buy. A novice's menu is more likely to become famous for crabcakes, roast rack of lamb, curried seafood, or crêpes than steak or roast beef. Marge Mitchell in Vermont served homemade soups, a choice of two or three each day, salads, and homemade breads. Alan Hooker in Ojai, California, has the waitress set a basket of assorted home-baked breads on the table before you order, then you choose from such selections as crab and saffron rice mounded into avocado halves and served with a fresh herb sauce, or pork tenderloin with Cointreau. Vegetables are an event, seasoned delicately with herbs, and salads are as colorful as a mixed bouquet—jicama (a crispy, cream-colored root vegetable), shredded beets, and carrots with greens, for example.

The Ovens of Brittany in Madison, Wisconsin, survives in a block with twelve other restaurants, with a menu emphasizing fat sandwiches filled with sprouts and avocado, hamburgers in several versions (Madison is a university town), and huge salads.

The Crab Cooker in Newport Beach, California, serves nothing but fish grilled over aromatic coals in mammoth cauldrons, fish chowder, coleslaw and, for dessert, pie or ice cream. A restaurant in San Francisco for years served hamburgers a hundred ways—the basic burger on buns or slabs of sourdough bread with a hundred-plus varieties of toppings. A roadside restaurant in North Carolina in the 1950s served platters of fried chicken, broiled chicken, or grilled chopped beefsteak with a mouth-watering variety of local fresh vegetables in season.

Your menu can be as individualized as your fingerprints, but test it, taste it, and try it on your cooks with every assortment of ingredients you might have to use. You know exactly how the food should taste and look, so supervise cooks or chefs closely so that they know how you expect a plate to look. This is the foundation of your reputation as a restaurateur.

Personnel

Cooks, chefs, salad men and women, dishwashers—everybody in a restaurant comes and goes. Your worst problems probably will be involved with personnel. In six years, David Yankovich, owner of Ovens of Brittany, cites getting and keeping qualified personnel as his number-one headache. Barbara Witt echoes this complaint, stating further that it is difficult to find "competent kitchen help!"

Many new restaurateurs serve as chief cook or know who the cook will be when they start plans for opening. Some, like Linda Spasato, start out managing the dining room, an unreliable cook leaves, then the manager takes over the kitchen, so does double duty with the help of unskilled and low-paid staff.

The highest-paid persons on the staff are the chef or head cook and the dining room manager or headwaiter. Partners or a husband and wife team may fill these two key positions. However, if you can afford to hire competent people to fill these jobs, they can be valuable. Professionals can advise you on setting hours, gearing for best money-making days and hours, planning economical use of convenience foods and equipment, and where and when to buy.

Finding competent, experienced kitchen and dining room personnel often is a problem. You might advertise in your local and nearby city newspapers and get just the right people or a half dozen or so misfits. You may find the ideal cooks and dining room managers for your style of restaurant and budget in newspapers or food-service journals. A few restaurateurs happen onto just the man or woman to direct the kitchen or dining room through blind luck, a friend who knows somebody, or a chance meeting.

The assistance of experienced help can save you from innocent errors, but don't let even the most skilled assistant take over. Talk with a prospective chef or dining room manager long enough to make sure he or she understands your dream of a restaurant. Your individuality gives a restaurant its freshness in appeal that even an experienced hand can't duplicate. A few restaurateurs, such as Alan Hooker in California, find training inexperienced helpers more satisfactory than turning over important jobs to persons trained in conventional restaurant operation.

Waiters and waitresses get a low base pay, but you may

be required to guarantee them minimum tips per hour. The style of the restaurant, menu prices, and clientele determine how much in tips they will make. These people, too, must be trained to express your style. They are your face to the world.

Certain labor-management practices are subject to regulations, federal, if your business is large enough, or state minimum wage laws, equal opportunity, and other labor laws. Hiring should be a thoughtful, investigative, and friendly job, but don't trip yourself up on questions no longer privileged. In prehiring interviews you can ask only questions concerned with work. But carefully check any references before hiring.

Training a new employee patiently and thoroughly can avoid misunderstandings and helps make a loyal aide of a worker. Your first few weeks with a new cook, waiter, or busboy demand much time and attention. A successful restaurateur constantly checks workers for competency and their dedication to the spirit you wish displayed. A restaurateur sees all, knows all, and almost needs eyes in the back of his or her head. While chatting cordially with a customer, the restaurateur knows how a dish looks on a tray being carried from the kitchen, how long a couple at a front table have waited for their order, and that a customer in the far corner is complaining to the waiter. The restaurateur soon learns to come to the rescue of a disgruntled customer or an unfairly treated waiter or waitress with as much tact as possible.

Open for Business

Incredibly, you're ready to open one day. Invite friends, neighbors, relatives, your lawyer, real estate agent, and anybody else you can find for the first preview meal before you open to the public. This gives the dining room and kitchen crews a chance to see how the menu, service, and other systems work. But that first lunch or dinner should not be overcrowded. The staff needs a chance to settle in, find out the routes around the kitchen to work smoothly, and how fast an order can be handled. You will have a chance to correct any glaring errors before you get rolling with paying customers.

When you open can be crucial. One restaurant in New York City almost failed because of two blizzards the first winter it was in business. You can't control the weather, but open weeks before the peak dining-out seasons (usually fall, winter, and early spring in cities) to allow time for the staff to learn their jobs. In the first weeks, too, you may change your menu, hire and fire staff a half dozen times. Items that sell well stay. You have to be heartless about your favorite dishes when you see that they don't appeal to diners or turn out to be too expensive in time and ingredients to be profitable. A menu item that gets only an occasional order simply isn't worth the storage space for ingredients and the chef's time to look up the recipe. You may find that tableside-tossed salads or flaming foods require too much serving time, and so are unprofitable. Or that a dish is impossible to present due to an irregular supply of an important ingredient. These items should be removed from the menu. Be critical in those first few weeks. Watch plate returns for foods barely nibbled at, and get rid of them or adapt them to customer tastes.

The entire menu may need major price adjustments. A dish may require longer preparation time than you expected. Food and labor costs may go up. You may be forced to produce your quiche more economically. Purchasing ready-to-fill quiche shells might save enough labor to keep your price competitive, or buying the prepared quiches might allow you to keep them on the menu.

During the first few weeks, you and your staff learn how to work together to organize a day's schedule to determine who opens up, who receives and checks deliveries or goes to the produce market, who totals up daily receipts and expenditures, who locks up and sets the burglar alarm (if you have one), who sets tables or starts the stock pot simmering, who has access to the cash drawer, and who checks restrooms to make sure the cleaning person left them clean, odor free, and supplied with towels, toilet tissue, and soap?

Acquaint all personnel with the location of safety equipment, fire extinguishers, main electric, gas, and water switches or turn-off valves. Post emergency telephone numbers and make sure somebody on duty knows where they are. You may operate for years without a medical emergency, but an emergency illness among customers or workers is unnerving. Your procedure should be thoroughly discussed with your attorney before you open your doors, and the necessary emergency phone numbers should be readily available.

Blowing Your Own Horn

Advertising, sales promotion, and publicity are important when you open and will go on forever. To open, you might take out small ads in your local newspaper or shopping news. You may have to continue this advertising or expand to other media in order to maintain a profit-producing flow of customers. Your ads should be factual, but enticing. Choose what is unique about your restaurant and emphasize that feature. Be honest about the mood of your restaurant, if you expect to draw repeat business from ads. Customers expecting sophistication will be disappointed if your style is casual; a high check may dismay a young family expecting a pleasant evening out. To be safe, advertise prices. Or without mentioning price in an ad, you might say, "home cooking in a country setting," less-expensive-sounding than "haut cuisine in a peaceful valley." If you're not good with words, get an ad copywriter to help. Some publications and radio stations will refer you to a copywriter or help you write an ad or commercial.

Most of the restaurateurs we interviewed report that the star of success first blazed brightly when they got publicity. Operators of one New York City restaurant, suffering after three months of a shortage of capital and slow business, were planning to close at the very time the restaurant critic for *Women's Wear Daily* reviewed their restaurant. Fashion designers, like pied pipers, led the crowds to the hot discovery, the restaurant thrived, and within three years the owners were planning to open their second restaurant, capitalizing on the goodwill and reputation established through publicity on the first.

Invite the restaurant reporters or food editors of newspapers, magazines, radio and TV stations in your area by telephone or letter or send them copies of your menu. Many critics arrive incognito and pay their checks, but invite the reporters to dine at your expense, if their organizations permit free dining. Ask these people for leads on other publicity, too. They often observe unusual facets of your restaurant that can be promoted in their own newspapers or shows or other media.

Often publicity strikes out of the blue, when you and your staff least expect it. Gear up the moment it does. Even mediocre restaurant reviews bring hordes of people, barring a blizzard or other act of God or man. Inability to handle the crowds can undo the benefits of the publicity. It is better to turn customers away cheerfully than to serve them poorly or have them jostling at the door, tempers fraying, while they wait for tables.

Don't underestimate the power of word of mouth. A word from a friend, cousin, or neighbor is worth ten thousand words of publicity to many diners-out. Your treatment of an individual customer can snowball into a dozen or more faithful patrons. A gastronome from New York City was impressed by the genuine concern of a restaurateur in Miami when she expressed disappointment with a dish on his menu. She was convinced he went directly to the kitchen to see if the cook was mishandling the dish. She tells her friends about the restaurant, the pleasant outdoor dining room, and the staff interested in your dining pleasure. Alan and Helen Hooker in Ojai had been in business almost twenty years and were doing well before a line was written about the Ranch House in any publication except the local newspaper. The movie crowd had discovered them, but kept the secret to themselves. Half the eating-out adventurers in Los Angeles were driving the ninety miles or so, and news of the place was transmitted principally by the grapevine.

Business Development

A good promotion can tide a restaurant over slow periods and sometimes add substantially to the income. Here is a grab bag of tried and true promotions; some may work for you:

Seasonal Promotions

Organize bus transportation to football games or other sports events, featuring brunch or supper before departure, with drinks aboard the football special, at a charge, of course.

For Thanksgiving, roast a small turkey for each group of six or more and carve the bird at the table.

For Mother's Day and Easter Sunday, advertise such special touches as a carnation for each mother accompanied by a child or children and an Easter basket for each child.

Celebrate St. Patrick's Day with corned beef and cabbage, Christmas with Old English or ethnic specialties popular in your region, Valentine's Day with heart-shaped cookies or ice cream molds, gingerbread men with children's names inscribed in frosting for birthdays.

Cultivating Clientele at Slow Hours

In retirement communities, promote early-bird dinners at a savings for retirees.

Near theaters and concert halls, provide before- and after-theater dinners at prices lower than regular dinners and with limited menus, plus complimentary transportation to the theater, if practical.

On Saturdays and Sundays, create special brunch menus, or have musical groups perform afternoon concerts.

Direct Sales Promotion

Distribute flyers, leaflets, and inexpensive copies of the menu to neighborhood homes and offices and post these materials on community bulletin boards in markets, community centers, or libraries, if permitted.

Participate in dining-club coupon-book promotions that offer specials at several restaurants to coupon-book purchasers.

Advertise with a coupon or special offer in newspapers, local magazines, or in premium books used as merchandising tools by banks or other businesses.

Advertise gift certificates and sell them at the cashier's or reception desk, especially at holiday times.

Internal Sales Promotion

Use table tent cards presenting a new dish or a new drink. Drink cards often are provided by liquor suppliers.

Promote food specialties or signature dishes on your slow days, with a special card clipped to the menu or the waiter or waitress announcing the day's specials.

In hunting or fishing areas, cook customers' game or freshly caught fish, charging for the service.

Serve a distinctive appetizer at the bar or at the table as soon as customers are seated, your specialty spread, cheese pot, hot hors d'oeuvre, or relish selection. Or serve an after-dinner drink of your choice at no added charge.

Stage food and wine festivals that express the style of your restaurant or highlight local color—crawfish in Louisiana, for example, shrimp in Biloxi, lobster in New England, local fruit or vegetable harvests. Or choose a region—France, Italy, or Germany, for instance—and combine the foods and wines of these countries for a promotional menu.

Contact local gourmet-food and wine societies or dining clubs and offer to work with their dinner committees for one of their meetings.

Engage a local wine expert to conduct tastings and seminars, paying him or her from admission or tuition fees. Or bring in a wine lecturer from a university to conduct wine tastings.

Decorate with local artists' works for sale or have periodic art shows.

Develop "calling cards" for your restaurant, unusual doggie bags with recipes for leftovers printed on them, place mats that children or adults may take with them, and, of course, matches and postcards to spread your name and telephone number for reservations.

Diversification

A logical start is with banquet service, club meetings, wedding, anniversary, birthday, and bar mitzvah parties. If you don't have a banquet room, book parties for days the restaurant is closed or partition off a section with folding doors or screens. If the grounds are large enough and landscaped, you might rent a tent when weather permits. Some rental companies supply heaters or air conditioners for tents.

You need reliable audio equipment and large tables for banquet service, available from rental companies, too. Nothing ruins a women's club rally or stag dinner like a microphone that requires constant tinkering.

For banquet service obtain deposits in advance, plus an agreement on the latest date for cancellation and minimum and maximum guest counts. The balance of the bill should be paid immediately after the party.

Retail and Wholesale Foods

These sales often develop from popular demand for your specialties. The Big Cheese in Washington sells its salad dressings and ice cream toppings. The Mimosa in New York City sells crêpes, quiches, and desserts, the crêpes in batches of five hundred and one thousand, to other food-service operators. Total your costs to see if you can set a competitive price for volume sales. For example, if your cook can produce crêpes at 5 cents each, you can sell them for 10 cents each for several hundred at a time, paying for any extra work involved in packing and selling them.

Catering

The kitchen meets legal sanitation requirements for food service and your staff is available, but you may have to invest in a delivery station wagon or van, additional staff with special training, and serving equipment as described in chapter 3. Try catering a small party or two before you make a major investment, since catering may turn out to be more trouble than it's worth. Nevertheless, Omar's Oasis in New York City, specializing in Middle Eastern foods, derives a portion of its income from catering private parties for representatives to the United Nations, and other restaurants find catering a profitable outlet for their services.

Other Retail Operations

A specialty-food shop or cookware shop is an ideal adjunct to a restaurant, since it often depends on the same suppliers as the food service. Other retail shops that have been combined successfully with restaurants include flower, antique, and gift shops. Customers are often drawn to the restaurant for the first time because of the retail shop. Promotion of the retail operation can be used to develop a mailing list for the restaurant and vice versa. Café Continentale sells menu items through the adjoining specialty-food shop, Cheese Plus, and ran contests in the shop to obtain names for promotion of the restaurant. Narsai David operates a charcuterie, wine, cookware, and specialty-food market in conjunction with his restaurant in Berkeley, California. Madeline Poley and Francine

Scherer had a neighborhood charcuterie in the Chelsea section of New York City before they moved and combined it with a restaurant in the Soho section.

The Country Store in Miami literally sells the decorations off the wall, many of them antiques. Once Upon a Stove, Sharma, and Chelsea Place are among the many restaurants in New York City that sell antiques as part of their restaurant operations. Trader Vic operates shops in his Polynesian-style restaurants, selling giftwares, from tiny fresh orchids in vials for a few dollars to smoke ovens at several hundred dollars. His Señor Pico restaurants in San Francisco and Los Angeles have Mexican gift shops. The Trader's cookbooks and others are sold in the gift shops.

Another Restaurant

Opening a second restaurant nearby or across town has all the problems (and sometimes more) inherent in opening your first. If you don't have loyal, competent backup help to manage one or the other place, you may be in more trouble than you want. However, if you have enough kitchen space and a well-trained staff, from the managerial level down, and established goodwill, you may piggy-back profitably in a second operation. You can take staff, prepared foods, and goodwill to the second location. The Soho Charcuterie uses the kitchen in Soho to supply some of the food for its second restaurant on East Fifty-seventh Street near Fifth Avenue in New York.

Crises

The very best management can't protect you from crises. The air conditioning fails on the hottest day of the year, the pump in the dishwasher is afflicted with a major disease, and the kitchen floor is flooded the same day that you find out your insurance premium has been increased 30 percent. Barbara Witt says that the major problem in the restaurant business is the aggregate of problems. "They swarm—sometimes like gnats, sometimes like bees. The small frustrations are relentless and seem more like one major problem. It isn't a difficult business, just a frustrating one."

Near the phone post phone numbers of repairmen and suppliers for each piece of equipment. Make friends of your repairmen. Give them lunch or dinner occasionally. Then maybe they'll come to your rescue at 6 A.M., if necessary. Make sure you or the person checking orders knows the delivery man for each supplier, too. When you need something the first thing in the morning, maybe he'll switch his route to help you.

Style

The menu, the wine list, the decor, the music, the use of space, the noise level, the dining room staff, the chef, your personality, and the tiniest details designed to tempt the customer make up the style of your restaurant. Don't get hung up on a mood or style that is too extravagant to maintain, and, above all, be guided by your market. Flexibility is essential, since markets change with trends and competition. You have to change with the tastes and times. A good manager stays alert to a changing market by dining in other restaurants occasionally, listening to customers' requests, reading the restaurant, food-service, and beverage trade journals, joining industry associations, and checking the ads and sales promotions of other restaurants.

Customers carry good news of your restaurant and return themselves if they feel comfortable, if the menu is unique, if you show warmth, and if the restaurant has an ambiance of its own. Customers expect you to maintain a standard of quality at a fair price. Any of these features, or a combination of them, will bring repeat business and new customers once you establish a reputation.

A few principles of style prevail, according to the class of restaurant you choose to operate. A restaurant needs a small foyer for early arrivals awaiting tables. Formal restaurants in most climates need coat checkrooms, but coatracks or hooks can be used in less formal spots. The attendant in one New York City checkroom adds a fillip to her service by sewing on buttons while customers dine. The hostess or headwaiter with a good memory for regulars makes good customers feel welcome.

The dining room as a total picture and the appearance of the exterior of the restaurant express your style. But be practical. One restaurateur stitched charming tablecloths and napkins as a feature of her decor, only to find they did not launder well. Keep in mind, too, the time needed to make replacements when the original cloths wear out. Selection from a restaurant-supply house or linen service may be more practical.

Printing of menus is expensive, and the larger, heavier paper very costly. If you use foreign terms on the menu don't mix French or Italian and English in one menu title: either *Fonds d' Artichauts* or Hearts of Artichokes, not Hearts d'Artichauts. Printers in some cities specialize in menus, and some have language experts on their staffs. Your market determines whether your menu should be all in English, all French, or French with English translations.

Low-cost alternatives to printed menus add flair to small restaurants. Write the day's menu on a slate or blackboard on an easel and have waiters or waitresses move it from table to table. Write it on notepaper and tape it to a Lancer's bottle or write it directly on the bottle with a china marker. The Grand Central Oyster Bar in New York has large blank menus with logos printed at the top. Seafood items are written in by hand each day after the buyer has chosen fresh fish at the market. A restaurateur in Tarzana, California, pins a handwritten menu to a muslin-covered dressform. It is difficult to read, but the headwaiter obligingly reads it to you in well-rehearsed French, translating for those who wish it in English.

Above all, have clean menus. Like spotted tablecloths or unkempt rest rooms, a grubby menu makes the restaurant look dirty, even if the kitchen is sparkling clean.

Fresh flowers are another token of quality. Even one or two inexpensive blossoms stuck in a wine carafe with a sprig of asparagus fern give the impression that the restaurateur took pains to get fresh foods, too. A small restaurant operated on a sheep farm in upstate New York has field daisies in ceramic jugs on each table, overlooking a field of Michaelmas daisies in bloom in July. Potted plants and growing things in hanging baskets are in vogue. They give a restaurant a fresh, springlike look, but they require care, so plan for it. Make sure low-hanging plants or pots that might topple are well out of the way of traffic lanes.

Presentation of food shows care or gross carelessness. A blob of sauce on the rim of a plate is inexcusable, and a waiter or waitress who shoves a plate in front of a guest as if it were so much excess baggage implies that the food is no good. Smudged silverware, bent forks, or cloudy glasses ruin the effect of carefully set tables. If silverware or glasses are smudged, check your supplier for better dishwashing detergents or water-conditioning chemicals.

Such details as uncomfortable chairs can hurt business. Nobody squirming on a hard chair is likely to linger for dessert and coffee. Try the chairs for comfort before you buy them, and if you are tall or unusually short, have other people try them. An irrepressible restaurateur in Newport Beach, California, bought high-backed straight chairs, turn-of-the-century vintage, at a thrift shop. The chairs are worn-looking and none match, but are sturdy and comfortable.

Wet lettuce and other greens are amateurish. Insist that greens be dried thoroughly so they don't dilute dressing. Sophisticated diners are put off by too much dressing, but some diners want gobs of thick dressing, blue cheese or red French. Know your customers' tastes!

Serve a good cup of coffee and good bread. Both are possible anywhere. Keep the coffee-making equipment clean, brew fresh coffee often and in the proper strength, measuring it instead of guessing. You'd be amazed at how good coffee can bring repeat business. Restaurateurs who feature teas, honestly brewed in a warmed teapot, with freshly boiling water and loose tea in a tea ball, can build a reputation on it. However, tea bags are more practical if tea is ordered only occasionally, but have the water boiling hot when it reaches the table or have the waiter drop in the tea bag when the water is boiling.

Good bread is one of the least expensive items on the menu, and almost every area has a local bread of high quality. Feature local bread—sourdough in San Francisco, the marvelous hard rolls and dark breads in New York, Cuban bread in Florida, fresh hot breads in the South.

Many pleasant restaurants avoid music. If you have music, it should suit your style—taped classics or ballads at low volume as background to conversation for a serene atmosphere, jazz or rock where the young congregate. Harpists play softly at Sunday brunch in several restaurants in New York. A chamber music group can provide pleasant accompaniment to dining, and strolling violinists contribute an air of glamour.

Never forget the charm and understated chic of simplicity for a sophisticated market. Don't be afraid to set polished wooden tables with chunky pottery bowls of fragrant bean soup, and good bread can make a name for you more surely than mediocre béarnaise sauce on a steak of dubious quality.

Choose your name to express the style of your restaurant. The Ovens of Brittany in Madison, Wisconsin, has a bakery in conjunction with the restaurant. "Don't be too cute," cautions Marge Mitchell from Hopi House in Arizona. Her first restaurant in Vermont was on Bakery Lane and soups were a specialty. She called it Bakery Lane Soup Bowl. "And before you buy expensive signs and have expensive logos designed, be sure you get to keep the name," she adds. "Most states don't allow two businesses with the same name, and when you register the name, it will be rejected if it is not original." Names with a suggestive sound are rejected by some authorities. A group of men starting a restaurant-bar in Manhattan Beach, California, applied for registration as the Oar House, but were turned down.

Your restaurant is operating, you're ironing out problems, and you've set a style. There are dozens of reasons customers aren't coming in droves, but one can be your style. If business is not up to expectations, examine your style, while you look at other factors. Style is successful only as long as it helps sell—and pleases you.

Chapter 6

The Art of Running a Cooking School

Cooking schools became the rage in the late 1960s and 70s. In almost every suburban enclave and dozens of city blocks and rural communities, women and men taught cooking—how to make flaky puff pastry, sauté golden tender veal scallops, or roast a rack of lamb (rare, if you followed the uptown pronouncements). The cooking school revolution was fired by thousands of women and some men who had time on their hands and couldn't find capable cooks for hire. It became fashionable to spend hours over a hot cooking school stove (or in some schools, leisurely watching an instructor slave at the stove) and come home to dazzle your guests with your version of your school day's lesson.

Some apt pupils started their own cooking schools, setting a few chairs for students in the kitchen. For a while it appeared that anybody who could bring off a little dinner party was teaching cooking. Some of these schools lasted a few terms. Some came on the horizon, shone for a year or two, then faded when the teacher lost her enthusiasm or dried up her own market by teaching all she knew to the thirty or forty people in her social circle.

As the 1980s approach, however, the best of the cooking

schools are flourishing, and a woman or man with the talent and drive can make a go of a cooking school. Hardly any successful cooking school in the country is hurting for students and some keep long waiting lists.

A born cooking school operator has three important qualities: a deep interest in cooking and food, a feel for teaching, and a good business sense.

Some cooking school operators we interviewed had experience in teaching. Julie Dannenbaum assisted in classes at the James Beard cooking school and with the late Michael Field in New York City before she opened a school in her home in the Chestnut Hill area of Philadelphia. Jane Salzfass Freiman had worked as an elementary school teacher, then took cooking lessons while an art dealer with Sotheby Parke Bernet, Inc., in New York, before she married, moved to Chicago, and opened her school.

Cooking school operators need an extra something, kind of a star quality, maybe a touch of chutzpah, to maintain the reputations that command the highest fees and long waiting lists. James Beard was an aspiring actor before he became a helper in an hors d'oeuvre catering business, then opened his famous cooking school.

Don't be scared off by high professionalism and acting lessons. Hundreds of schools succeed modestly, sometimes as much as you want them to, in a home kitchen. And most of the teachers love every minute of the teaching. It's the preparation for classes, the dealing with assistants who themselves may turn out to be prima donnas, and the figuring and accounting that become chores.

From Cottage Industry, Cooking Schools Grow

Most cooking school directors we interviewed started schools in their kitchens by popular demand. Irena

Chalmers, who operated La Bonne Femme in her home, then in a church-owned house in Greensboro, North Carolina, describes her beginnings: "I had a dinner party and somebody said, 'I'd like to do that.' I said I would show her how. Two or three days later she came to my house and I showed her. That developed to four people, then six people."

Julie Dannenbaum, whose present Creative Cooking, Inc., in Philadelphia draws students from all parts of the country and who is in constant demand as a visiting instructor in schools in the United States and Europe, "never intended to open a cooking school." She had been deeply involved in cooking for ten or fifteen years, commuting to New York City to take courses with noted teachers, to Europe for courses at the Cordon Bleu, with Richard Olney and Simone Beck, and had worked in the kitchen of the late Dione Lucas's restaurant, the Egg Basket.

There were no cooking schools at that time in Philadelphia. Friends asked her to teach. Other teachers advised, "Don't teach your friends." Just the same, she opened the school in her home, and the number of her pupils has grown far beyond the few friends who first urged her to start classes.

Beatrice Ojakangas, a food writer with credits in almost every magazine that buys free-lance food articles, was helping in a charity rummage sale in her home city, Duluth, Minnesota, when coworkers asked her to teach them cooking. Within a few weeks, she was teaching part time, continuing her writing and work as a consultant to a cookware firm.

Jane Freiman's beginnings were more elaborate. Mrs. Freiman was given a cooking school as a present from her husband. "When we moved to Chicago in 1974 my husband said, 'You're going to teach cooking,'" she recalls. He had the kitchen in the house they bought remodeled and equipped to her specifications, and she was in business, in a city that already had several good cooking teachers giving courses.

L'Académie de Cuisine in Bethesda, Maryland, an affluent suburb of Washington, opened big time in a commercial building in 1976. A businessman with a love of gastronomy, Donald Miller, and a classically trained chef, François M. Dionot, are partners in L'Académie, and Miller and another partner operate a cookware shop on the first floor of the building. The school started with an investment of about $100,000 after market research had indicated the concept was valid.

Come into My Kitchen

Imagine six, eight, or twelve pupils milling about your kitchen, spilling milk or dropping eggs on the floor. Who will clean up after them? Not they! Cooking students want only the fun, not the drudgery, of cooking. Teaching cooking is not just whipping together a smooth hollandaise and having students *Ooh!* and *Aah!* at your legerdemain.

Do you have enough space? Too many cooks not only spoil a broth, they frazzle nerves with their chatter and jostling.

Julie Dannenbaum had a terrace enclosed in which students could sit while she demonstrated. The terrace was adjacent to the fifteen-by-twenty-foot kitchen. A table was placed between the kitchen and the remodeled terrace so each student could get a clear view.

Jane Freiman estimates that remodeling the kitchen and the enormous basement for storage space in the mid-70s cost $20,000. This included all equipment. She purchased a used dishwasher, and a refrigerator came with the house. A second refrigerator and freezer were purchased for the storage room. In the seventeen-by-seventeen-foot kitchen she has twenty-four cooktop burners and sufficient counter space for every student to work under her guidance. She limits enrollment to ten students per class.

A sit-down lunch or dinner, the table properly set and appropriate wines poured with the food, climaxes each lesson. The dining room the Freimans use for private entertaining seats ten comfortably.

The Ojakangas family designed their house for themselves. The first floor is one room combining cooking, dining, and living area. The kitchen is large enough to permit participation by eight to twelve, and the students lunch on the food they prepare.

Abby Mandel rents one location in Chicago and one in a suburb for her school, Machine Cuisine. She divides classes about equally between a community house in Wilmette, a suburb, and the International Institute of Food and Family Living in Chicago. She also teaches lessons on contract in department stores, such as Marshall Field (Chicago), Bloomingdale's (New York City and suburban stores), Nieman-Marcus (Dallas), and Burdine's (Miami).

Ms. Mandel specializes in adapting classic recipes to the use of the latest equipment, as the name of her company implies. She has six assistants who participate in lessons, recipe development, and writing for publication. Abby writes a monthly column for *Bon Appétit* magazine, articles for other publications, and has written a cookbook, *An Abby Mandel Machine Cuisine Collection.*

Ms. Mandel, who holds a master's degree in social work from Smith College, began cooking for a living after bringing Julia Child to Chicago for a benefit demonstration for Smith College. Public interest ran so high that Ms. Mandel became a gourmet consultant to a small specialty-food

chain in Chicago, and her school evolved from these amateur beginnings.

Irena Chalmers limited her classes at home to twelve
but preferred eight. "Everybody had to be comfortable,"
she said. She moved to other quarters, a church-owned
house, since neighbors were complaining of too many
cars parked on the street during the cooking lessons in her
home, but she maintained the same limit in the other
location.

Keep It Legal

Zoning becomes a sticky problem if you teach at home.
You might tutor one or two students, with no violation of
residential zoning regulations, but a school with more
students may clash with zoning laws.

Mrs. Dannenbaum's lawyer advised that she would be
in trouble holding classes in her home and suggested that
school profits be donated to charity to avoid legal compli-
cations. For the short time that she taught at home, she
paid all expenses, including a wage for her time, food, and
other expenses, and then contributed the profit to charity.

She predicts regulations will get tougher. "There are
too many little ladies teaching cooking over Bunsen burn-
ers in their houses, and they'll have a problem when somebody gets ill or gets hurt from a knife or hot fat on the
stove." Cooking teachers should check insurance needs
carefully. Mrs. Dannenbaum says her insurance was $4 a
year when she started, $400 in 1978, and she expects it
to be $500 in 1979.

In some states and counties, a cooking school is subject
to health inspections, and if the school trains professionals,
it must meet board of education regulations and obtain a
private educational institution license in most states.

If you remodel a building for use as a cooking school,

you must have safety, fire, and other building code inspections. L'Académie de Cuisine, which teaches professionals as well as amateurs, had to obtain twenty-three different licenses. In some states, even the credentials of your assistants are scrutinized by officials to adhere to the law.

Getting Students

Attracting students is less trouble once a school makes a name for itself. Many cooking schools turn away prospects each term. Waiting lists are kept and brochures mailed to prospects each season. If a cooking school is started by popular demand, usually the first course or two will be filled. Drawing students afterward, however, takes an effort.

Cooking school directors report that publicity gave their schools their kickoffs or strong boosts. A major article in *The Washington Post* filled the classes of l'Académie de Cuisine immediately, and word of mouth from those first students has created such a waiting list that Miller and Dionot, the partners, feel they need more than their thousand-square-foot space for classrooms for prime-time lessons. Julie Dannenbaum's first classes were mentioned on a radio station in New York City, and she has had waiting lists for the fourteen or fifteen years since.

In her case, publicity and word of mouth continue to supply students. "I get a phone call on Monday morning because somebody went to a dinner party Friday and the hostess said she learned to make the dessert or prepare the entire menu in my school," reports Mrs. Dannenbaum. "Or husbands phone and sign up their wives."

Metropolitan newspapers list cooking schools once or perhaps twice a year. Keep in touch with the department that handles this directory, since newspapers usually make each school responsible for accurate information. The directories carry the name, address, and telephone number of the school with a brief description of the curricula and styles of classes. A major newspaper article on your school is more valuable, of course, but most newspapers do only one article on a school over a period of several years, unless there is a major change that is considered newsworthy. Radio and TV shows, magazines, and neighborhood newspapers also offer opportunities for publicity.

Irena Chalmers was asked to do a weekly TV show in Greensboro within a few months after her school opened and never could accommodate the applicants who came to her as a result of her mentioning the school on the show occasionally.

Some cooking schools take small ads in gourmet-services directories in food sections of newspapers or local magazines. Neighborhood shopping news or a community bulletin board may accept mentions at low cost or no cost.

If business is slow, a school director might ask prospects to sit in on a lesson for a small fee. Observing a lesson before registering also gives potential students a chance to see if the school is to their taste.

Sales promotion brochures distributed by mail or through a local neighborhood association or merchants' association can attract students. Real estate agents sometimes provide a packet of neighborhood services to new home buyers. If one in your neighborhood does this, supply him with your brochures.

Your exposure as a lecturer in other schools and for charity benefits and as a guest demonstrator in department stores or cookware shops can help build student interest.

Writing cookbooks and food articles for magazines builds your reputation. Membership in wine and food societies and civic organizations provides good contacts to help bring in students.

Credentials

Your credentials and those of your instructors enhance the image of your cooking school. Irena Chalmers and Julie Dannenbaum attended l'Académie Cordon Bleu in Paris—and Julie studied at almost every well-known school in New York—before opening their schools. Mrs. Dannenbaum's school now is as prestigious as some she attended. Her former students now teach in many states.

François Dionot studied at l'École Hôtelière in Lausanne, Switzerland, virtually a passport to the kitchen of almost any restaurant in the world, and worked as a chef in hotels and restaurants before founding l'Académie de Cuisine with Donald Miller. Other cooking school operators are home economists, some with teaching experience in high schools. Many are simply passionate home cooks putting their flair for gourmet cuisine to profit.

Cooking school teachers continue their education, in Europe, New York or California, or other cities, to keep abreast of trends in cooking and introduce new foods to their students. Julie Dannenbaum considers travel essential to learning about food. Jane Freiman and dozens of other teachers study in Europe during the summers.

Teaching in other schools before you open a cooking school has the added benefit of giving you a taste of the work involved. You will find out whether you really enjoy teaching and also obtain insight into the business operation of a school.

What to Teach

The cooking school craze of the 1960s and 70s followed closely the phenomenal success of *Mastering the Art of*

French Cooking, coauthored by Julia Child. The book revolutionized attitudes about cooking in this country. At first, most of the schools taught so-called classic French cuisine. Mrs. Dannenbaum and other fine teachers still do. Professional schools also emphasize classic techniques and foods, though now there are subdivisions of these, cuisine minceur, the less rich French cuisine that gained attention in the 1970s, and specialty subjects, fish and seafood soufflés, for example. Until the Child book, cooking schools here had primarily taught basic American kitchen chores. One teacher in Los Angeles, now retired, taught three generations of brides in some families, showing them how to cook for husbands and families on the maid's nights off.

Now cooking schools vary their curricula. Mrs. Ojakangas teaches Cuisine I, which includes crêpes and soufflés. Cuisine II, gratinéed dishes; and Cuisine III, which is advanced classic techniques. She also teaches one course each on lake trout—popular in Duluth—picnics, barbecuing, pastry, and bread. James Beard formerly offered a single lesson, just before Thanksgiving, on carving.

A sociologist by training, Abby Mandel had never worked before she got into cooking. She was chairman of a benefit for Smith College for which Julia Child demonstrated cooking. The benefit was such a hit that Ms. Mandel went to France to study cooking herself, at La Varenne, in Paris, then apprenticed in a Parisian bakery, La Poilane, and in several restaurants, including the three-star Taillevent. She first went to work for a market chain, then started her cooking school. She continues to spend at least three weeks each summer in France to bring herself up to date on chefs' work.

Cooking schools adapt their curricula to new trends in food and cooking.

In the 1970s, teachers began giving special instruction

on food processors as their use in homes increased. Teachers often give special request lessons. One summer a teacher in a New England resort was dismayed to have a student ask for a lesson on clam hash. The teacher was not familiar with this dish, which the middle-aged pupil remembered from her childhood. The teacher practiced secretly, working from instructions her Yankee neighbors provided, until she developed a foolproof formula. In a few days she showed the class how to make clam hash.

A course or lesson devoted to wine is on the curriculum of some schools. Guest lecturers in wine appreciation add sophistication to your classes. Wine and cheese tasting as a lesson or course will have appeal in communities where specialty shops bring in new varieties of cheeses and wines. These courses are especially interesting to men.

Ethnic cooking classes are popular almost anywhere. A teacher with a well-rounded curricula sometimes adds an Italian, Chinese, or Greek class to the schedule. Women from the Orient or other cultures with intriguing cuisines have made businesses of teaching and writing about their foods.

Listen to the questions in class, ask students occasionally what courses they'd like that you don't offer. Observe the promotional literature of other schools. Stay on top of the market.

I DISAGREE How to Teach

Julie Dannenbaum and Irena Chalmers feel strongly that demonstration is the best way to teach. "I love to demonstrate," says Mrs. Dannenbaum in her forceful manner. "I think the students learn more. They miss too much in participation classes since each group is doing something different."

Mrs. Freiman and Mrs. Ojakangas advocate participation just as strongly. "Students have to feel when a sauce or dough is right," says Mrs. Freiman. She demonstrates a technique, then two partners share each job at their assigned cooktops or work areas. People who've never made bread, for example, have to feel when the dough is right, Mrs. Ojakangas believes.

L'Académie de Cuisine conducts both demonstration and participation courses. This is true of many schools offering courses for hobby cooks as well as professionals. Madeleine Kamman's school in Newton Center near Cambridge, Massachusetts, teaches both demonstration and participation courses. Her serious students return to assist at the school or start their own lessons or go to restaurant kitchens. One teacher in New York City provides private cooking lessons, exclusive participation for one, with the instructor guiding every stroke of the knife or whisk of the sauce, at a price, of course: $150 or more per lesson.

Cooking techniques represent only about one-half of the success of cooking lessons, Mrs. Dannenbaum explains, "You almost have to make it look like a magic show.

"I prepare everything ahead and set it on baking sheets for each recipe. Nobody wants to see me chop six cups of onion. I chop all but one onion before the students arrive. If something takes a long time to cook, I put that on early, so that when the students eat, I pull the cooked food from the oven and tell them it was started earlier. The organization of a lesson is very important."

Entertainment value takes high priority with students. A teacher must learn to use his or her hands so that procedures are not hidden from students' view. In many schools, a mirror is angled over the demonstration table so that students get a cook's-eye view as well as front-row-center view of the techniques.

A dish should be rehearsed before it is shown to a class.

A cheese fondue that doesn't blend properly may be a jolly joke for a teacher with a national reputation, but an embarrassment for a teacher beginning her climb to fame. If you change the brand of cheese due to poor supply or for any other reason, test the recipe to make sure the cheese melts as you expect.

Helpers should be carefully chosen to work tactfully with you and the students, without upstaging you. Even gracious cleanup workers add to the mystique of a cooking school. One teacher had a middle-aged student who was apprehensive that she would make a mess when separating an egg. She insisted that the other students turn their heads during her first try. Instructors and helpers must pamper such whims. To end the anecdote happily, the middle-aged novice separated her first egg with no mishap, so became a class champion at the technique.

Mrs. Freiman regards patience as a prime requisite for a cooking school teacher. One of her first students was a retired man who did not even know how to measure. She tactfully showed him, and he has returned for refresher courses two or three times and now does much of the cooking at home.

A cooking instructor must be generous with information and time, thinks Mrs. Dannenbaum. Students ask "everything under the sun." Lessons should be planned to allow time for questions and unhurried answers. Mrs. Ojakangas says students ask details about menu planning, as well as the cooking covered during the lesson.

Each student is given recipes for the dishes taught in the lesson. They may be typed and reproduced at a copying center for students to keep in notebooks or file. A basic recipe such as a soufflé or béchamel sauce may be demonstrated in one or two versions, with variations for students to try at home included on the recipe sheets.

The finale of the lesson is lunch, dinner, or, in some

schools, just a tasting. The meal is a teaching situation, with appropriate wines and a discussion of other wine choices that would be appropriate. The table is set properly, sometimes elaborately. Mrs. Diane Wilkinson in Atlanta says the majorty of her students expect a formula for a dinner party from each lesson and for a course to yield a repertoire of dinner menus. The tasting and meal service is especially valuable to novices learning how to organize dinner parties.

To vary class routine, some cooking schools invite guest lecturers. Among those who appear often are Mrs. Dannenbaum; John Clancy, the former chef for Time-Life cookbooks and author of a book on baking; Jacques Pepin, chef, restaurateur, and writer for *House and Garden* magazine; and Philip Brown, the writer and cooking teacher from Pasadena, California. Mrs. Dannenbaum says guest lecturers have become so expensive, she plans to discontinue using them.

Some teachers organize field trips to meat and produce markets where students are given practical instruction in selecting top-quality products. A course in ethnic cooking may be climaxed by a dinner in a good restaurant specializing in the style of cookery being taught. Students are shown how to order and given a tour of the restaurant kitchen. A restaurant visit should be arranged well in advance, so that the chef and restaurant manager are alerted to presenting the food as beautifully as possible.

Time

A cooking school can be a part-time job, more soul-satisfying than profitable. By necessity, cooking schools are seasonal—the terms coinciding roughly with conventional school terms. Most students won't come during vacation and holiday times. Irena Chalmers fitted in two six-week courses between September and very early December, before the holiday rush. Her classes started again after New Year's, and she usually gave three six-week courses before the end of May.

Beatrice Ojakangas confines teaching to two weeks a month, since she gives priority to her family and to writing food articles and other work that yields higher income. However, she considers teaching students valuable for testing out what she presents to readers. Seeing students fumble with dough helps her to know how much detail to write into a bread recipe for an article.

Julie Dannenbaum started part-time in her Chestnut Hill home, but the school snowballed into a full-time business. She now spends twelve months a year at teaching and related activities such as guest lecturing and travel. Jane Freiman teaches roughly eight months, but travels and continues to study in Europe during the summers and writes a few articles each year.

Cooking schools in resort areas run seasonally only, and some teachers in cities transfer their schools to country houses in the summer. Other schools offer special holiday cooking courses, usually one- or two-lesson courses, in December to fill slack time and meet the special demand of novice party-givers.

Some schools offer only daytime classes. Others provide evening classes for business people. One New York teacher does a lunch-hour class for men only. The men cook and eat their own lunches in two hours.

Helen Worth

The classroom time represents just half the work, if that much. All cooking teachers we interviewed reported that the preparation before a two-hour class required at least two hours, plus shopping. Some time is needed, too, to have equipment maintained and replaced when it wears out or becomes outdated. In off-seasons, brochures are written, printed, and mailed, registrations and deposits taken. A popular cooking school director works from waiting lists. Due to the cost of printed materials and mailing, Mrs. Dannenbaum revises her lists each year, another time-consuming job.

The operator of a new school must develop mailing and telephone lists. These lists can come from membership rolls of charity groups, social or country clubs, and civic organizations that allow use of their rosters, from the local social register, if there is one, or you might purchase a list from a local specialty-food shop.

Money

Cooking schools, especially at home, require a relatively small capital investment as compared with other businesses, but also yield low income unless run on a full-time basis with efficient use of the space, equipment, and staff, day and evening, twelve months a year.

The cooking school operators we interviewed invested anywhere from a few dollars to the $5,000 Julie Dannenbaum invested in a lease and equipment when she moved her school from her home to a small building in Germantown near Philadelphia in the middle 1960s to the $100,000 l'Académie de Cuisine reports investing in 1976. L'Académie was founded as a full-time business, and professional chefs as well as amateurs are trained there. Three or four classes are conducted daily and evenings, and some on Saturdays and Sundays.

Mrs. Freiman had a $20,000 kitchen to start, paid for by her husband, and spent a couple of hundred dollars more on brochures and other promotional materials. Irena Chalmers says her investment in the early 1960s was minimal, even after moving to her second headquarters. Mrs. Ojakangas made no large investments, but teaches only part time, and the number of students is sharply limited by the space in her home.

Purchasing and maintaining cookware can be a considerable expense. Cookware should be of the best quality, say school owners. Equipment such as range tops, ovens, and refrigerators is expensive. Some school directors use equipment on consignment, which means the manufacturer provides it for testing and demonstration in the school. Mrs. Dannenbaum says she makes no deals with manufacturers "because you're then at the mercy of the manufacturer when he wants to photograph."

Some teachers give entire courses on equipment. Abby Mandel offers individual courses in microwave and food-processor use. If purchased, specialty equipment becomes very expensive, though many manufacturers are anxious to provide them. Irena Chalmers admits the cookware for her school in Greensboro was extravagant, since she used all copper and hired help to keep it polished. Though she sold her school in the early 1970s, she still uses copperware and Le Creuset in home testing.

Setting prices for cooking classes was "a wild guess" for Julie Dannenbaum. She geared her price of $10 a lesson to those in New York, and Philadelphians said nobody would pay that much. They paid, and by the end of her first year she had a waiting list of eighty. She now charges up to $125 for a three-lesson series and $350 for the one-week crash course for out-of-town students. In addition to tuition, the students make their own arrangements for travel and living expenses in Philadelphia.

Jane Freiman charges $125 for a three- or four-lesson series, but says at least half that goes for food costs. For a class of ten students the food runs about $80 per lesson, going as high as $125 when the subject is lobster or another high-priced food.

Mrs. Ojakangas charges $65 for a three-lesson course "because that is about all people here will pay." She doesn't lose money, but the profits are slim. She feels she "feeds the cooking school expense and profits into the machine," which encompasses her writing and work as a consultant.

L'Académie de Cuisine charges $180 for a series of eight classes for amateurs, and $675 for a series, or $25 per lesson for professionals.

Students who reserve for a course and then don't come create financial problems for a cooking school. No-show registrations are especially disastrous in classes limited to only six or eight students, since their places are difficult to fill on short notice. Many directors require enrollees to sign contracts and pay deposits several weeks before sessions begin. The contract should spell out the latest cancellation date and the policy on refunds, such as one-third up to two weeks before beginning of the session, no refunds afterward. Your policy on makeup classes should be clearly stated. Some schools arrange makeup with another group for classes missed.

Jane Freiman broke even her first year on expenses and now makes a little money thanks to writing on the side, but has never paid herself a salary. L'Académie de Cuisine makes a living for three families. Mrs. Dannenbaum paid herself a salary from the start and never lost money, but she says "nobody will ever get rich running a cooking school."

The spin-offs from a reputation as a cooking school operator, however, can be profitable. Julie Dannenbaum did a movie for a fee for the Campbell Soup Company and is in heavy demand as a guest lecturer in this country and abroad at handsome fees. Irena Chalmers made little money with her cooking school, though it was her first love affair with cooking for profit. Her most profitable ventures have been books and brochures, one of which sold almost a million copies, and the publishing company, Potpourri Press, that she and a partner formed as a result.

A cooking school operator has certain tax advantages, travel and equipment expenses that can be deducted as legitimate business expenses. A CPA keeps up with changing tax regulations. Ask your accountant before counting on a trip's being deductible or before taking utility expense deductions for a school operated in your home. Not just any joy ride qualifies as a business expense.

Many cooking school operators we know are in the business not for high profits but for the joy of teaching and the prestige it offers.

Rewards

Operating a cooking school will win you fame, if not fortune. A cooking school operator becomes the resident expert, sometimes a national and international expert, on culinary affairs. A cooking school serves as a springboard to writing, working with food companies and restaurants for fat consultant's fees. You can work at it almost as much or little as you wish.

Irena Chalmers expressed the richest reward she felt: "I enjoyed it! It was my own; I had created this school myself." She admits she organized the school to fill her spare time, not for income. Dozens of cooking school operators would agree with her.

But others such as l'Académie de Cuisine and Julie Dannenbaum's make a profit or use the school as the road to other ways of cooking for profit.

Chapter 7

Getting in on the Gourmet-Food and Cheese Shop Boom

Remember grandma's chicken salad, meaty chunks of chicken, about half as much celery, chopped sweet pickles or olives, and the whole thing bathed in fresh homemade mayonnaise? Today's young gastronomes will remember a salad of chunks of chicken in a lemon, curry, ginger, and garlic mayonnaise, chopped chutney, celery, green grapes, and pecans (from the Montana Palace, a catering and fancy-food takeout shop on Madison Avenue in New York City), or any number of variations made by fancy-food-shop recipes all over the country.

Fancy-food boutiques will be the gourmet boom of the future. This is the opinion of such authorities as Julie Dannenbaum, the noted cooking school director, and T.G. Koryn, president of Lankor, Inc. a mammoth fancy-food import and domestic sales company in Carlstadt, New Jersey. Previews of this facet of food merchandising in the 1980s are showing in the lineups at gourmet shops in New York and other cities at breakfast and lunch hours, then again after office hours. Women and men tote home shopping bags crammed with pâtés, specialty cheeses and

breads, smoked duck, salads, and other delicacies. Entrepreneurs are opening and succeeding at fancy-food
shops in areas formerly viewed as meat-and-potatoes or
grits-and-gravy country. Driving along a street in a southern city, one sees a block-printed sign announcing a store-
front shop simply as "Indian Market," and a few blocks
away a similar sign marking a "Syrian Bakery."

Some specialty-shop chains and franchises (Hickory
Farms with cheeses, sausages, and accompaniments, a few
health-food groups) have done well in certain locations
with good management. Most supermarkets are stocking a
few fancy-food items, and the ready-to-serve delicacies in
the delicatessen sections of a few would dazzle the palates
of world-traveled epicures.

Who Is Your Customer?

The most loyal shoppers in specialty-food markets are
women working outside the home, couples and live-alon-
ers, and the women and men who are into the gourmet
cooking craze. Specialty-food shops get customers from
both ends of the culinary spectrum, those who hate to
cook or don't cook and the cooking fanatics. These groups
are growing.

In 1978 more than half the women between nineteen
and fifty-five years of age were working outside the home.
A woman going back to work changes meal and other
housekeeping patterns in dramatic ways. She cooks less,
she almost never has time to bake special treats, the family pitches in more, they eat out more, and serve more
prepared foods. After a hard day at the office or plant, a
housewife or househusband stops to pick up ready-to-
serve food for dinner, and the gourmet boutique offering
such choices as boeuf bourguignonne or veal breast
stuffed with rice and pine nuts is competing for this trade.

Working wives want weekends off, too. A gourmet meat shop in New York packs Friday get-away bags. The customers' choices of thick prime steaks, frozen chicken kiev, or saltimbocca and individual quiches are packed in bags and labeled with the customers' names. Shoppers stop en route to the train or curbside in their cars to pick up their bagfuls of goodies to feed weekend guests and the family.

The singles and the doubles boom has spawned market innovations in all sectors of industry, and food as dynamically as any. When buying for one or two, it matters less that Greek salad or heat-and-serve lasagna from a takeout shop costs three times the cost of homemade. Income for many singleton and doubleton households is high, and the cost of homemade soars when the expense of leftover feta or other special cheeses and fresh vegetables and olives that age ungracefully in the refrigerator is considered. Another group, couples whose children have grown and left home, feel they've had their cooking phase, from pablum to hamburgers by the dozen. They patronize specialty-food shops happily, rather than home-cook for two.

The love-to-cook group from Atlanta to Phoenix, Seattle to Miami, is poking around everywhere for such oddities as lemon grass for Indonesian sambals or star anise for Chinese dishes, seasonings they'd never heard of in 1970. They're the adventurers, too, who try the most exotic cheese the storekeeper can get and the latest tidbit to serve with cocktails.

Two social changes are bringing in customers, too—the comeback of picnicking and the takeout business lunch. A handsome, good-tasting box lunch is almost as predominant at summer concerts in Hollywood Bowl in Los Angeles and Central Park in New York as home-cooked chicken and potato salad. Box lunches at desks or shared with clients in conference rooms make cash registers jingle in some fancy-food shops in urban centers.

John Rusnak at Capitol Hill Wine and Cheese Shop has sent box lunches to a meeting at the White House, and gotten a note of thanks from President Carter. He regularly sends lunches to congressional committee meetings. New York publishing bigwigs pass up some of their luncheon haunts occasionally to have stylish sandwiches and salads brought in from such spots as the Taste Bud near their offices. "It's less hectic to eat in the office," said one publisher. Some secretly agree that the food brought in from an innovative shop is less hackneyed than the restaurant fare that they've lunched on for years.

How Do You Start?

A specialty-food-shop owner has to love food, but he also must be a born retailer, according to Ira Horowitz, owner of the Taste Bud in New York City. Emanuel (Mike) Margarites was virtually born to the business. He worked in his father's market in Greenwich, Connecticut, then after he was out of college, worked with a national supermarket chain before he returned to Greenwich to make the Gourmet Galley of the family market. John Rusnak started from scratch, as did Horowitz. Horowitz made money almost from the day he opened the Taste Bud in January 1978. He had worked as a film editor for seven years, accumulating the capital to go into business. John Rusnak and a partner, who has left the business, are former Christian Brothers. They pooled their resources of $35,000 to open the Capitol Hill Wine and Cheese Shop in Washington, D.C., in 1974. Though business was brisk from the start, overhead and starting costs forced them to borrow money to keep going a few months later. Trish

Sclater-Booth and Emmy Smith started a fancy-food shopping service after a chance conversation on a park bench while their children played nearby. Their business required almost no capital—about $200 for printing price lists—no warehousing, and no help. They take orders by phone from customers for foods from gourmet shops in New York City, pick up foods Thursday mornings and deliver Thursday afternoons.

Gourmet cookware and gift shops offer many of the joys and problems of gourmet-food shops. Ruth Henderson, who operates a cookware shop with a few food items in New Milford, Connecticut, started the business, the Silo, to use some of the space on the family's weekend farm. She invested about $12,000 and, even though the space was available, she says it wasn't a penny too much. "Don't undercapitalize!" is her first advice to beginners. Before her marriage to conductor Skitch Henderson she was a fashion model, but hard business figures fill her pretty head. She also cautions against "piddling away profits" with too much help. The Silo is open only six or seven months of the year, so she employs one full-time helper and temporary help seasonally. An owner must be able to do any job, and in her case she cleans, takes out garbage, and keeps daily accounts, when necessary. At off-seasons, she refurbishes the shop, buys for the next season, and she and the helper unpack and check orders as they arrive—a detail some novices neglect. Even the most reputable shipper has a slipup in the shipping room occasionally, and a short order or damaged goods that are not salable can eat up your profits.

Russell Vernon of West Point Market in Akron, Ohio, says, "Spending money just because you have it can be a big mistake." In 1978 he installed a kitchen to expand the prepared-food line. He purchased used refrigeration equipment, saving $2,000 for similar fixtures new. Vernon, who has built up enough equity in his business to afford or finance almost any improvement purchase he deems necessary, thinks cautious buying is essential to good business in the fancy-food field. He is an inveterate traveler, visiting specialty-food shops everywhere he goes. On a trip to New York City he commented on the simple but attractive transformation in the premises of a new food shop, Dean and Deluca, on Prince Street, achieved at minimum expense. "They used lots of paint, the least-expensive thing you buy in decorating," he said. "Used properly, paint can do wonders for a few dollars."

Vernon inherited the West Point Market from his father, and his experience goes back to teen years when he worked with his father. Nevertheless, he is eager to share his opinions with the beginners. The three major causes of failure, he says, are undercapitalization, a poor site, or a store that is too large for the stock.

He estimates $35,000 to $50,000 as a minimum starting capital in the late 1970s, depending on such variables as store space, local property values, and the labor market.

A Good Site

Specialty-food shops depend heavily on drop-in trade and impulse shopping. It is not traditionally a business that draws customers across town for a weekly shopping foray. The shop must fill the neighborhood wants and needs, especially in takeout foods.

"You put a fast food Mr. Hero in a blue-collar area, not in a high-income area," observed Russ Vernon. On the other hand, it is hard to sell pâtés and charcuterie to a clientele accustomed to hot links and breakfast sausage or wieners and bologna.

Look for a location with potential buyers passing the door en route to work or daily shopping or near enough to detour to your shop, if you are in the city. In a small town, suburb, or rural area, good parking and access routes are essential, and because of the nature of a fancy-food shop a location outside the central market area may require vigorous advertising and promotion to get it going and maintain a profitable business volume.

A primary advantage of specialty-food shops is that they require little space. One fancy-food-shop operator says fifteen hundred square feet is the minimum for display, sales, and a kitchen, half the space devoted to the kitchen. However, Ira Horowitz operated the Taste Bud for several months in nine hundred and fifty square feet, plus a basement for storage. Russ Vernon thinks the stock you plan to carry should be mentally placed on shelves before going to much more than fifteen hundred square feet, or you may be burdened financially with too much space. He thinks two thousand square feet is too much for a cheese shop, in most cases. But if cheese will be combined with wine, prepared fresh foods, and enough other items, you might use two thousand square feet efficiently.

Before choosing your location, survey the competition. If there is another fancy-food shop in the area, can you provide better food, better prices, or unique items that the established store does not sell? You may find unexpected competition in supermarkets and ma-and-pa markets, too. Study the deli departments of nearby supermarkets and restaurants that promote takeout business and the stock of any corner-store–type markets. They can kill your business if you don't offer specialties they can't handle. Today's supermarkets and small markets are cashing in on the gourmet food and no-time-to-cook markets, too, and in ways a small-time shopkeeper can't meet. You have to sell something better or different or offer extra service.

Before selecting your site, check zoning and necessary licenses. A preparation kitchen must meet local sanitary codes, and the kitchen and store probably will be inspected periodically. In a few areas, however, you may need only a food-store sanitation check, if the kitchen is used primarily for slicing meats and cheeses, assembling sandwiches and salads, and no cooking. Local health regulations also monitor the sanitary conditions of markets.

The shop must be equipped with refrigerated display cases (wipe them sparkly clean if you purchase used equipment), open shelves for food in cans and jars, plus counter space for the cash register and any business forms such as order blanks. Some shops provide a few tables or a counter for customers having coffee and pastries or sandwiches. In fact, selling samples of house blends builds sales for take-home purchases of coffees, pastries, salads, and sandwiches. In some areas, tables or a counter require a restaurant license, so find out before you build in a counter or buy chairs and tables. A few shops in cities, where eat-in requires a restaurant license and inspection, post signs over the takeout counter, "Sandwiches [or food] cannot be consumed on premises."

How to Do Business

Before you open your doors, set up lines of supply. As soon as you set up your business or even get business cards printed you can attend fancy-food trade shows, regional and national, and thus see and sample foods you plan to buy. Before that, addresses of suppliers can be obtained from such organizations as the National Association for the Specialty Food Trade. Don't overlook local suppliers. Housewives preparing their specialties, quiches, cakes, cookies, pastries, soups, salads, and almost any food you can imagine can provide your most distinctive delicacies. The proprietor of one fancy-food shop in New York City buys almost every fresh food he sells from housewives gone professional in their kitchens. Some restaurants in your area may sell soups, salads, or salad dressings in portions suitable for your sales volume. Once you're open, and reordering, salesmen will beat a path to your door.

Mike Margarites of the Gourmet Galley in Greenwich, Connecticut, says wise buys can mean the difference between success or failure. "Years ago a retailer had enough margin so he could make mistakes and not get hurt," says Margarites. "But no longer."

Margarites tastes every item he buys and shops as carefully as a penny-pinching housewife. He buys the smallest order possible, a case or only a half dozen items, on a new food to "feel the pulse of the consumer." In 1978, he was watching the prices on imports inch up, then leap up as the value of the dollar skidded. When the price hit a high mark he set as the limit on the basis of what he thought the customer would pay, he cut the item out of his line. "No matter how affluent the customer is, there is a cutoff point for her," he says.

House specialties—the "home"-made salads, sandwiches, pâtés, or other delicacies—should be given a trial run before you open, and before you set prices. Calculate the cost of ingredients, your and any helpers' time, and packaging. That is the cost to you. Most gourmet-food-shop operators mark up salads, prepared main dishes, and other perishables 50 to 60 percent to cover any waste. This markup applies to in-house production and food from suppliers. Cheeses and less perishable meats such as sausages and any frozen items usually are marked up about 33⅓ percent. John Rusnak at the Capitol Hill Wine and Cheese Shop sets the price on a box lunch by totalling the cost of the labor (six minutes of a worker's wages, for example, if that is the average time required to assemble the lunch), the retail cost of the foods in the lunch, and the packing materials. That makes the cost of the lunch.

His box lunches in red-white-and-blue-checked or pink-gingham-checked boxes range in price from $2.99 to $4.99 each, with some less expensive for two or more. Rusnak delivers lunches, party platters, and other items at no added charge for orders of $10.00 or more.

The inspiration for a fancy-food shop often is an urge to show off your salads, quiches, or pastries, so allow time in your schedule for the necessary kitchen work. Ira Horowitz, however, is a non-cook. He has a deep interest in foods, but his motivation to give up film editing for his shop was to get into the retail business. He organized the business, hired a good cook to supervise the kitchen, and operates successfully with consistent high quality from his kitchen, supplementing the line with foods from suppliers that meet his standards.

Before you open and regularly afterward, foods must be arranged attractively on shelves and in refrigerated chests. It is important to have shelves filled, even if you tuck in a basket of fruit or low arrangement of dried flowers to fill out a shelf when stock is low or a shipment is late. In a temporary shortage of an item in a fancy-food shop we visited, the owner had put a large script-lettered card announcing, "Sorry, the shipment of mustard is delayed in the shipping strike. When it arrives, you'll see it here."

Ruth Henderson in her cookware shop says it is important to keep staple items in their accustomed places so regular customers know where to put their hands on them. But, for variety, she changes certain slow-selling items from time to time. "The pottery that sold only a few pieces sitting on a table at the back may go by the dozens when we move it to the floor on the other side of the shop." The same principles hold for a fancy-food shop—staple, steadily moving items should get their niches and stay there. Foods that sell less often or in spurts and bursts might do better if moved to a special display occasionally.

A small fine-food shop can be operated with a small staff, maybe only one full-timer in addition to the owner and part-time sales help for rush hours. To hit the best selling hours, it may be desirable to open before 8 A.M. (coffee and breads to take to work) and stay open until 6 or 7 P.M. (take-home orders). This means you have a long work day, part of it with no help since employees cannot be expected to work more than eight hours. So to cover the long hours, you may need another full-time helper. Otherwise, part-time sales help at rush hours may fill your needs. Also track sales and labor costs of the added morning and evening hours for a few weeks to judge if the extended sales day is profitable.

If lunch business is heavy, standard sandwiches might be spread and wrapped during the slow morning hours. Some salad making or cooking also might be done at this time. Immediately after the rush for coffee and rolls in a gourmet shop in the IDS Center in Minneapolis, the saleswomen begin packing lunches—cheese or cartons of yogurt, bread or a meat sandwich, and fruit in small trays covered with clear stretch wraps. They are refrigerated for lunch buyers to pick up, pay for, and carry away as they flee for a good seat around a decorative pool.

Russ Vernon, in Akron, regards competent help as one of the most important features of a specialty-food market. His market is larger than most fancy-food boutiques, so his staff is much larger, and to free himself for the creative activities he feels essential to the business, he hires eight department heads, giving them heavy responsibility for their domains (meats, produce, prepared foods, etc.). Other workers are recruited carefully for their interest in customers and doing a good job. With the cooperation of the employment office at Akron University, he recruits and interviews prospects for part-time jobs, just as the large industrial employers in Akron do. He taps the housewives' labor pool, a rich source of part-time employees, by advertising in local help-wanted ads: "Housewives wanted——." Many of the women itching to get out of the house or needing a few spare dollars are ideal employees for a specialty-food shop, thinks Vernon.

"We arrange their hours so they can be home when the children get there, and a good housewife in our store is an asset," he explains. "When a customer asks about a certain food, the housewife-saleswoman is understanding and helpful. She has been there!"

Trish Sclater-Booth and Emmy Smith, with their A La Cart fancy-food delivery service, have no help problems. They so far have shared taking orders, shopping, and delivery amicably. In 1978 they were interviewing prospective helpers, since if they expand or work out vacation schedules for themselves, they will need helpers.

Sales Promotion

The very best location with thousands walking by daily can't make a fancy-food shop go. To start, and maybe continuously, you must lure customers into your shop. John Rusnak credits much of his success to his years of experience as a fund raiser with the Christian Brothers, which gave him a practical insight into persuasive newsletters. "You can make it if you have a tremendously creative mind," he says. "Otherwise, it's just plenty of sweat and hard work." Rusnak distributes a Capitol Hill Wine and Cheese Shop newsletter periodically, reporting on new cheeses and other foods, wine news and "buy" suggestions, such as a list of hostess gifts in various price ranges in one newsletter. Rusnak has been unusually successful at getting articles and column note mentions in Washington newspapers and magazines.

He and Russ Vernon at the West Point Market in Akron

value exposure at civic affairs. Capitol Hill Wine and Cheese's truck—the shop's logo giant size on the sides as a built-in advertisement—also parks at a permitted spot at outdoor music and arts festivals and sells lunch boxes and sandwiches. At a benefit festival in Cleveland, Vernon provides cheeses for tasting and buying, the market's cheese-tasting guide, and shopping bags carrying the message home with the festival guests.

Vernon and Rusnak are among the few specialty-food retailers we interviewed who also handle wine. The combination is not permitted by liquor regulations in some parts of the country. The markup on wines is usually controlled, although the somewhat smaller markup is offset by the glamour and one-stop shopping convenience the wine offers. Both shops conduct wine seminars and similar promotions as goodwill builders.

The smaller shop owner, sometimes with less experience or time for sophisticated public relations techniques, still can do much to build a loyal clientele. The young owner of the Silver Palate, on Columbus Avenue, in Manhattan, stood at the doorway of his tiny shop one Saturday morning, when working women are likely to browse for food. He cheerfully discussed the menu items, his prep kitchen (around the corner), and where he buys his breads. His shop is a few blocks from the meadow in Central Park where summer concerts are presented. A bold poster done with a felt-tipped marker announcing "Concert Picnic boxes" was taped to the window.

A stylish sandwich or lunch deserves a stylish name, thinks John Rusnak and other shop owners. Rusnak's lunches are named and described in mouth-watering detail. The Madison is "A delightful combination of braunschweiger, Finni Lappi cheese, French bread, choice of wine or nonalcoholic beverage, fresh fruit or chocolate chip cookies, knife, glass, napkin & after dinner mint, smartly

boxed. $2.99 + .08 tax (for one); $5.98 + .16 (for two)."
The Hamilton description reads: "Are you weight con-
scious? This is for you: Jarlsberg skim milk cheese, Darbo
skim milk cheese, health salad (choice of cole slaw, potato, cucumber & onion), fresh fruit, knife, fork, napkin &
after dinner mint. $3.89 + .31 (for one). Double for two."

Rusnak distributes his newsletter containing lunch selections, new items, suggested gift packs, and other information to customers who order regularly, in the shop and
to nearby offices. Other gourmet-boutique operators distribute promotional literature in nearby apartment buildings or homes. Where permitted, such materials can be
tacked to community bulletin boards or supplied to rental
agents to distribute in packets for new tenants or to real
estate sales people who provide neighborhood information
for home buyers. Send complimentary box lunches to
these people as a persuasive sample of your services.

One Great Dish

The very existence of a specialty-food shop demands
unique foods—at least one, sometimes an entire list.

A few fine home cooks gone professional started with
one great dish, and a few prepare or sell little more. Miss
Grimble's cheesecake is known from one end of Manhattan to the other, and in all the boroughs. Her home shop
on Columbus Avenue now has been expanded to sell other
desserts and pastries, but the flagship item still is the
cheesecake.

The Famous Corsicana (Texas) fruitcake was so successful it went mail-order, and the family that started selling the fruitcakes more than seventy-five years ago makes
a year-round business of fruitcakes.

The Red Herring, in Greenwich Village, in New York,
means just that, pickled herring in six or eight ways, plus

gravlax prepared according to the owner's—Paul Sand-blom—mother's recipe.

Smithfield ham producers have brought the art of one great food to a fine point that has made a high-quality standard profitable. To end a friendly southern rivalry over which is the "best" country ham, the smokehouse operators in Smithfield, Virginia, banded together and set their standards: the pigs must be peanut fed and the hams cured with certain ingredients. But most important, to be called genuine Smithfield, the ham must be smoked and packed in Smithfield. There still are fine country hams in many areas, but none can be called Smithfield except those cured by four major producers in Smithfield.

Chapter 8

Succeeding in the Mail-order Food Business

In the 1930s Cordelia Knott made preserves from a newly developed hybrid blackberry, the boysenberry, and sold them at a roadside stand on the family farm in Buena Park, a rural community just south of Los Angeles. Almost a half century later the Knott family, the original Cordelia Knott's children and grandchildren, operates a nationwide business, the boysenberry and other foods sold mail-order and in their gift shop in the third largest amusement park in the nation, based on those first jars of Mrs. Knott's preserves.

Pierre and Deland de Beaumont virtually shop the markets of the world (often via fancy-food shows and importers) to fill their Brookstone catalog with such delicacies as ragout of wild boar meat from Poland, barley sugar from England, and white asparagus from France (one of their most popular items). The Brookstone catalog reads like an epicure's pantry inventory, though Mr. and Mrs. de Beaumont's mail-order business permits them to live in the rural charm of Peterborough, New Hampshire.

A mail-order business can be carried on from any hamlet in the United States and a rural or small-town location offers certain benefits. Warehousing and packing-house facilities are less expensive to rent. The labor pool, especially for temporary help, may be rich.

If you cook foods for mail-order sales, local sanitation laws may be less rigid. The inspector, at least, is a neighbor and can become a friend in helping you meet health specifications.

A small-town postmaster, lawyer, accountant, or insurance agent often becomes a friendly ally in helping you do business.

There are hundreds of direct-marketing (what you and I call mail-order) success stories, some of them true and some embellished by lively imaginations. But mail-order remains one business that a small-timer can go into with a small investment. If you are dedicated to hard work, handling detail, and willing to do the grubby work such as packing and pasting on mailing labels and have a skill for organization, you've a future in mail-order.

You need a touch of chutzpah, too. BeeBee Gow of Gow Bee Farms in Katy, Texas, started a letter: "This isn't modest, because I don't know how to be modest and sell a product." Her letter went on to extoll the gourmet honeys that are the foundation of the family business, available by mail-order as well as in gourmet shops.

Your Line

The Gows in Texas got into honey production as a hobby, then made a business of it. Alyne Stroud's mail-order jellies and preserves are a spin-off from her roadside café in Union Church, Mississippi. She began selling the home-made delicacies that restaurant patrons enjoyed with hot biscuits and rolls, then went mail-order, by popular demand. She stocks the classics, apple jelly, strawberry, peach, and blackberry preserves, but handles local delicacies such as huckleberry and muscadine preserves, and her most popular items are the novelties, camellia, rose petal, and hot pepper jellies.

Menuchah Farms Smokehouse in Salem, New York, started in 1975 with bacon, turkey, and the traditional smoked meats, and added such novelties as smoked duckling. Maxine Cook in New Hope, Pennsylvania, who has operated the Farmhouse from her kitchen table for more than fifteen years, started with one food item, Irish whiskey cake, and her mail-order business has been expanded to aprons and pillows rather than other foods.

Frank Lewis Schultz in Alamo, Texas, ships one item only, Ruby Red grapefruit, and his are called Royal Ruby Reds, thanks to the special inspections he and his workers give the fruit. The Ruby Red is a delicious freak of nature that grew unexpectedly on one branch of a tree in a grove in the Rio Grande Valley. In New England and Michigan, mail-order entrepreneurs ship maple syrup and candies. In Georgia, their specialties run to pecans and country hams. In Iowa, mail-order foods feature popcorn, and in California, olives, homegrown nuts, and citrus fruits.

Two Texas companies, the Collin Street Bakery in Corsicana, and Mary of Puddin' Hill in Greenville, ship fruitcakes and little more. In Hawaii, mail-order usually is fresh pineapples, papayas, macadamia nuts, and macadamia, coconut, and pineapple cakes.

If you're a catalogue freak, which many Americans are, you would be amazed at some of the big businesses that started as small family businesses. Some of the best known are the Wisconsin Cheese Makers Guild in Milwaukee and Pfaelzer Brothers in Chicago, Illinois (prime meats and other specialty meats, poultry, and game).

How to Start

Presumably you have a product in mind, a home-baked or homegrown food, unique or better than anything in the retail market or other mail-order catalogues. Read as many catalogues as you can get your hands on and study the mail-order sections of magazines that carry mail-order food ads. While you're reading, study the writing style catalogue listings use.

The Direct Mail/Marketing Association (see chapter 13) maintains a library of catalogues on loan, if you cannot obtain a cross-section of catalogues for study.

Most importantly, check catalogues for foods competitive with yours. Mail-order depends on the individuality of your food or foods. It might be wild elderberry jam or tomato preserves. You might establish a mail-order business with fancy nuts or an exotic selection of spices to appeal to the gourmet cook. Good sellers also include fruitcakes and confections that home cooks don't care to bake themselves. Good mail-order sellers usually are good gift items, too. The consumer and business gift orders keep some mail-order companies financially sound.

Once you have established that your food or foods are unique, you've tested their shipability (with cartons designed for them), and are convinced they will bring in orders and repeat business, you're ready to set up your procedures, costs, and how to tell the world you're ready for orders.

First, decide how you will ship. Set up an appointment with your local postmaster to discuss what you plan to ship. Post office regulations on packaging for shipping usually are posted, but you can clear up any doubts by talking with the postmaster or his representative. Also he may give you advice about which days and hours are best for shipping, about arrangements for delivering your parcels at the loading dock if you have a large volume, and about other details. He also can assist in estimating mailing costs and delivery dates. If your foods are suited for holiday giving, ask him what your final shipping date should be for guaranteed delivery.

You may choose an alternate shipping method, an express or delivery service. However, many of these services do not deliver to all areas, so you may use a combination of the U.S. mail and a delivery service. Your most economical use of a delivery service may call for a once-a-week pickup or drop-off at its shipping station.

Delivery services such as United Parcel Service will be found under that heading in the yellow pages of the phone directory. Listed under Freight Forwarding are companies that handle large items. A mail-order shipper might use such a service for packages in large cartons for one area, with a parcel delivery service arranged for at the destination.

Have a package designed (or a carton in stock may work) to protect each item or combination of foods in shipping. Maxine Cook, at the Farmhouse, in New Hope, Pennsylvania, said she shopped for months at paper and packaging suppliers for packaging that would protect and enhance the looks of her Irish whiskey cake before she found the proper carton at a price she thought reasonable.

Mail or ship a few test cakes or jars of honey or cheeses to friends and relatives. Ask them to tell you frankly how they arrived, when, and, as a mini-market test, if they liked them.

Who Will Buy?

There are two ways to start—by buying mailing lists and mailing out price lists or brochures or by advertising in regional or national magazines. An ad provides an inexpensive test for your business. Later you may buy mailing lists, but after a few years you will develop your own.

Menuchah Farms in upstate New York has been in business with its smoked meats and poultry since 1975 and never taken out an ad, yet the operators maintain a very receptive mailing list, consisting of customers brought in by publicity in New York City newspapers. Mrs. Cook has depended on local publicity and word of mouth, one satisfied customer telling another. She builds her mailing list for semiannual newsletters from names of persons who order.

Printing a price list or newsletters can be relatively inexpensive if a process such as photo offset is used. You or a member of the family with good handwriting might handwrite the price list for a few items, describing each to whet the reader's appetite. A catalogue such as Harry and David's in Medford, Oregon, or the Wisconsin Cheese Makers Guild can run into thousands of dollars because of the price of color photography, production of color printing plates, and printing. However, an attractive and well-designed catalogue is a necessity when you grow to a line of several dozen items.

Who Helps?

Mail-order foods are a seasonal business, usually heaviest before the holidays. This is an asset if you plan your life around it, but a handicap if you must fit mail-order between other jobs. One shop in New York City that once distributed an elaborate catalogue each fall has discontinued it. The owner said he and his father, who theoretically had retired from the business, spent sixteen and eighteen hours a day at the store from November 1st through Christmas Eve attempting to fill Christmas orders. Longtime customers are reluctant to admit an order given December 15th no longer can be packed, shipped, and delivered before Christmas Day. This man could not find competent help to toil in a grubby shipping room.

Maxine Cook works completely alone, cooking, cooling cakes, then packing them. She attempts to have all her Christmas orders out by December 1st. She writes her newsletters, keeps books, bakes for the mail-order business and a few local pastry and dessert orders, and takes her packages to the post office for mailing.

Daniel Rosenblatt, a psychologist, and Charles Morris Mount, an interior designer, operate Menuchah Farms Smokehouse with the help of a supervisor and less-skilled help. Their business operates year-round, though they don't ship in the warm months due to the perishable nature of smoked meats. Heaviest demand is at Christmas, Thanksgiving, and Easter, however.

Mary and Sam Lauderdale operate the Mary of Puddin' Hill bakery in Greenville, Texas, with eighty-one employees, some at the heavy fruitcake-baking season—August to December. They often hire older housewives who can't type or take shorthand, but want to go to work. The Puddin' Hill fruitcake batter is so stiff that it must be worked by hand, so there is a need for women with the feel for baking in their hands. Their helpers range in age from fifty-five to seventy-eight, and one woman retired at age eighty-one a few years ago!

Fresh-fruit shippers usually have a heavy demand at holiday times, but the citrus season will extend into March or April, due to the harvesting of fruits, and gift peaches, apples, and plums require heavy summer work.

How Much Do You Make?

Markups on mail-order foods usually are heavy, 50 percent or more, to cover the special service in packing and shipping it. The customer will be more tempted to order for gifts if postage or shipping charges are figured into the listed price. The post office can weigh and price packages for each zone in the United States and abroad, if you wish. Any sales tax (usually applicable only within the state) should be mentioned so the customer can make out a check or money order to cover the entire cost of the order.

Diversification

Once you've established a mailing list for your cake, honey, fresh fruit, or other food for mail-order, it is easy to expand, especially if you have space or can rent packing shed or warehouse space inexpensively and can obtain part-time or full-time help.

A related food, of course, is a logical offshoot. Mary of Puddin' Hill ships slicing fruitcakes in three sizes and a few years ago diversified to bite sizes, called Little Puds, and now chocolate-dipped bite sizes.

Other items might be simple, too. Maxine Cook in New Hope, Pennsylvania, went to easy-to-ship gift items when she diversified. She is known for her "hug-me" pillows, velvet and lace boudoir or sofa pillows, and angel aprons.

A local or your own cookbook (spiral bound or paperback, produced by a printer so it can be sold for $5 or less is best) is a natural, and books are easy to pack and ship.

If you ship jams, jellies, and preserves, it is easy to extend your line to chutneys and relishes, packed in the same size jars so you can use your usual cartons in three-jar lots or assortments.

A successful mail-order firm can branch out into a gift shop or fancy-food shop, which Mary of Puddin' Hill has done in Olla Podrida, a shopping mall near Dallas. Some sell their wares in markets. Menuchah Farms Smokehouse has sold smoked meats to restaurants and fancy-food boutiques from the start. Mary of Puddin' Hill also opened an antique shop and small restaurant adjoining the bakery a few years ago.

Mrs. Cook sells breads and fruit tarts locally and caters parties in Princeton, Philadelphia, and Trenton, New Jersey, occasionally.

It's a Big Business

The Direct Mail/Marketing Association estimates that $60 billion worth of goods are sold annually through direct-mail marketing. Food, of course, is a small percentage of this giant business. More than a million people are employed in direct marketing or related jobs. DM/MC describes it as "one of the fastest growing means of selling and communicating with customers, prospects and clients."

Yet you, Mrs. Professional Housewife, or whoever you are, looking for an exciting new career, can find your niche in this beehive of activity.

A few years ago mail-order had a low credibility rating with consumers. A few ruthless or inept operators had spoiled the good image of mail order the way one bad apple will spoil a barrel of good ones.

The image has improved. Many customers have been surprised to have an instant refund when goods are returned. Most mail-order firms send postcards informing customers when orders are unavoidably delayed and many enclose response cards with deliveries. Fresh-fruit shippers find this bolsters their reputation with the customer and also provides valuable information. The card of one shipper asks the recipient if the fruit arrived in good condition, on what date, and for any comments.

If you're a novice in mail-order foods, keep these systems in mind. If a carton is not protecting the jelly jars sufficiently well, the first broken shipments can help you correct the problem. Customer-response cards also help establish your reliability rating. A new person in the business cannot afford slow orders or damaged goods, and arrangements for adjustments must be made when you start your business.

Though you ship a few hundred pounds of cake, several hundred gallons of honey or maple syrup a year, you're in a big business now, a competitive business—but a fascinating business, too.

Some mail-order cooks carry on friendly correspondence with their regular customers, swap children's snapshots and other such old-time warmth. Mary and Sam Lauderdale simply adore a couple who ordered five pounds of fruitcake once a month for several years—to feed their pet raccoon. The Lauderdales thought the raccoon had gourmet tastes—and loving owners.

Chapter 9
Free-lance Cooking and Food Planning for Hire

As a lark, twenty-four-year-old Rozanne Gold applied for the job as chef at Gracie Mansion, the New York City mayor's residence, and got it. For $200 a week and room and board in the mansion, she prepared meals and party food, on a budget limited by the economy drive of Mayor Edward Koch. A few years earlier Miss Gold graduated from college with a teaching certificate, but she chose cooking as a career. Her training consisted mainly of "hanging out" in restaurant kitchens, catering lunches in a law firm's dining room, and working in a catering kitchen.

Nancy Immel, sous chef at the Pump Room in Chicago, changed her aspirations from liberal arts to culinary arts while she was in college. She was an uninterested liberal arts student in Boston University. Casting about for an alternative, she knew she liked to eat, so thought cooking might be her future. She enrolled in the Culinary Institute of America at Hyde Park, New York, where many chefs train, graduated and worked as chef of a small restaurant

141

in the East, taught a food course, and then joined the Pump Room kitchen staff.

Cooking for wages offers practical benefits such as health and other insurance, worker's compensation, and paid vacations without the risks of running your own business. You get to dabble in the kitchen at somebody else's expense, though most cooking jobs require sharp budget limits. There is an aura of glamour in cooking downstairs for the powerful and famous upstairs. Certain jobs for pay offer outstanding opportunities for helping—school food and consumer service, for example.

Sarah Hoge, who supervises social events at the Museum of Modern Art in New York, is paid to make parties run smoothly—order food, plan the seating arrangements, and the myriad other details of good hostessing. Her guests demand—and appreciate—the finer points of party giving. Mrs. Hoge had no special training in catering or any other angle of parties, except in her own home, where she entertained beautifully, when she was persuaded to help with receptions, teas, and dinners at the museum for three months. Fifteen years later she was still at the job, ordering food and centerpieces and attending to the work that makes a party go smoothly.

Museums, art galleries, and many small colleges and prep schools employ social directors or hostesses to see that parties are run properly. A woman or man with skills in organizing home parties and working with temporary cooks, waiters, and other helpers might find such a post as a temporary sideline or full-time staff position. In some museums or educational institutions, social event supervision is assigned to a public relations assistant or administrative assistant to the director. Anyone with secretarial or office management skills and a deep interest in overseeing perfect parties might seek out such posts. The principal requirements for organizing semipublic parties is a knowledge of food or sources of information when special menus are needed, protocol—especially in situations when foreign or government dignitaries are guests— familiarity with catering, florists, and other party facilities in the community.

However, social director or hostess for a museum may be a one-of-a-kind position in a city or town. The most abundant opportunities in cooking for hire fall into four major groups: (1) in restaurant, catering, and other food-service establishments; (2) in government-financed food service such as schools or institutions, including hospitals and homes for the aged; (3) in consumer and retail food service; and (4) in government-sponsored programs in nutrition education.

Jobs in restaurants or catering services are yours almost for the asking, due to the trend to eating outside the home and the shortage of diligent workers in this field. The unskilled jobs most easily available to untrained personnel don't pay much and may require late or split shifts or other odd hours. A person who gets an unskilled job often has an opportunity for rapid advancement, if he or she will stick with the job and exhibit interest and the ability to learn.

One young man financed jazz guitar lessons by working in a famous restaurant kitchen in Denver. He started as a dishwasher, was promoted a few weeks later to salad man, then dessert man (preparing parfaits and other simple refrigerator desserts). He worked on holidays and until early morning after an annual banquet, but the generous daytime hours off allowed time for his music lessons. A junior editor, tired of magazine pressures, began baking desserts in the evenings for a restaurant in her neighborhood. She eventually left her editorial work for a job as a cook there. When the restaurant opened a new dining room, she was made chief cook, overseeing several helpers.

Cecile Lamalle Woicik, a New Yorker, represents the hundreds of women who create careers with their culinary triumphs at home as the inspiration. Mrs. Woicik as a wife and young mother was known for her chic dinner parties and her skills as an imaginative cook. So when she sought self-fulfillment, cooking was clearly her field. She took a course at the hotel and restaurant management school of the New York City Community College, worked part time in a restaurant and as a teacher in a cooking school. She wrote and sold a few articles in magazines. When she was divorced and needed a full-time job, she became food editor of *Restaurant Business,* a trade journal.

Mrs. Woicik had operated a cookware shop in the barn of her summer home and had thought of other ways she might go into business. But the security of a salary made her feel comfortable. Working for hire gives a beginner a golden opportunity to find out if he or she really wants to cook as a career.

A person with no experience or training will first work in menial, even unpleasant, jobs, as a rule. If you plan to make restaurant work or catering a lifetime career, training is certainly an asset. The ultimate is a course in one of the great European schools such as l'École Hôtelière in Lausanne, Switzerland, or a degree in hotel and restaurant management from one of the good American universities. A few Americans manage to become apprentices in European restaurants. Vocational training schools in almost every state teach catering, restaurant management, commercial baking, and other skills of food service. Ask your local or state board of education for a list of such schools. Certain schools such as the CIA, which the Hyde Park institution calls itself, and Johnson and Wales in Providence, Rhode Island, have national reputations that virtually guarantee gifted graduates good jobs from the day of graduation. Cornell University and the University of

Michigan schools of hotel and restaurant training are famous, but many other state universities and technical schools give you a solid background in professional restaurant techniques and an entree to an ever-growing market for trained personnel.

A person seeking a simpler, less time-consuming job away from home might choose school food service. Mrs. Brown came out of her home kitchen in a small Alabama town to start the first school cafeteria I (JV) knew. She cultivated the qualities a person in this kind of job needs —a love of children, patience to put up with their finicky tastes, plus an ability to cook good food and work with unskilled helpers. Mrs. Brown and dozens of her sisters took pride in serving well-prepared foods, and Mrs. Brown had the finesse of never letting on which children were eligible for the free milk available to the poor. One school cafeteria director who was famous for her pineapple fritters and eggplant at the Miami (Florida) High School had a yearbook dedicated to her.

If you are really interested in serving inexpensive and nourishing food as attractively as limited funds allow, work in a school cafeteria can be a boon. The hours allow a mother to go to work about the same time children leave for school. Vacations and holiday times coincide with children's school breaks. Almost every state offers low-cost or tuition-free courses in nutrition, food preparation, and other aspects of food service to school lunch employees. The pay is moderate, but supplements a family income without the high costs of child-sitting, and often the job is in the neighborhood so you avoid long and expensive commuting. The jobs available range from cooking, dishwashing, setting up cafeteria service, and dishing up foods onto plates as children make their choices to management positions, usually for people with experience.

Esther Coley, who retired in the early 1970s as supervisor of food service in more than forty schools, is a success story of all time. Mrs. Coley, a black woman, was concerned that her daughter's school in Willowbrook, a suburb of Los Angeles, had no hot lunch facilities in the early 1940s. Mrs. Coley prevailed upon school officials to start a lunch program. She was told there were no funds available. Mrs. Coley used her own savings to start a lunchroom, using a kitchen on the school grounds. She soon was making the lunches pay for themselves, the goal of most school lunch programs. Mrs. Coley also learned the procedures for applying for aid from the federal school lunch program and became an authority on preparing foods donated by the U.S. Department of Agriculture in ways the children would eat them. Meanwhile, the school district was consolidated with others, and when she retired thirty years after she served her first school lunch she supervised lunches in forty-two schools, never losing sight of the fact that good food made good lunchroom manners and perked up listless appetites.

Consumer service departments of supermarkets traditionally are staffed by graduate home economists. However, a few chains have pioneered employing "experienced consumers," housewives who have served their time choosing from the myriad products in supermarkets, standing in check-out lines, and hassling with meatcutters to get special cuts. Julie Grayson at Ralph's Markets in California was widowed with children to support. She assessed her qualifications and decided her best talent for a salary would be in consumer service. She bravely approached the Ralph's Markets personnel office, was hired as an assistant in the consumer service department, under supervision of a home economist. The home economist left for another job. Mrs. Grayson had shown such skill for handling customer questions, complaints, and compliments that she was put in charge of the department. She now handles phones and letters with part-time secretarial help and a telephone-answering device when she is out of the office. An expert shopper, she follows a customer question or complaint from the department manager in a store back to the buyer and, if necessary, to the manufacturer. Not necessarily a gifted cook, Julie answers how-to-cook questions with the aid of a library of cookbooks. Several other chains are employing housewives with shopping expertise to counsel shoppers, in the markets or by phone.

Food-demonstration services offer another opportunity for a woman with a knack for cooking to work with shoppers. The demonstrator is employed through an agency, much as the model agencies or temporary clerical agencies. A manufacturer or grower employs the demonstrator to offer a new food product, or a taste of a fresh fruit to customers pushing carts through the market. The demonstrator sets up a display, any simple cooking equipment such as a hot plate that is needed, and a supply of the food being shown, at a spot designated by the store manager. The demonstrator cooks any sausages or offers cubes of cheese or fruit or paper cups of the new soup to customers, urging them to buy.

Names of the food-demonstration services are listed (under that designation) in the yellow pages of city telephone directories. Jobs are temporary, usually one day at a time, and pay is moderate. However, good demonstrators, those with a gift for showing tidbits neatly and for selling the customers with one bite and a good line of chatter, are in high demand. Food-demonstration services also staff display booths at some food and market convention exhibits.

The expanded Food and Nutrition Education Program, an activity of the U.S. Agricultural Extension Service, is the largest consumer aid program in which an "amateur" can become involved. Program aides live in the neighborhood and counsel families on public aid in choosing foods for best nutritional value, planning and cooking meals. Program aides knock on doors to reach their clients. Aides are hired, trained, and supervised by extension service home economists, and for many aides, these are their first jobs. In 1978, salaries ranged from the minimum wage to $6 an hour, depending on length of service, responsibility given the aide, and the location; more than fifty-five hundred aides were working in twelve hundred cities, counties, and Indian reservations. In the first five years of the program, more than twenty-two thousand were employed. Numerous aides, starting with no more than an eighth-grade education, have finished high school, and a few have enrolled in college or gone on to better-paying jobs in hospitals or senior citizen nutrition education programs. But to many aides, the greatest reward has been seeing families improve their meals within the limits of their income, cooking skills, and kitchen equipment.

Almost all the businesses mentioned in other chapters offer opportunities for the amateur itching to put cooking skills to work for profit. Cooking schools need helpers with demonstration abilities. If you have an urge to teach, but no taste for business, try setting up a course in your local adult education school, a senior citizens club, a youth recreation center, department store, or cookware shop. You will be paid a fee or salary, and the school or shop provides the facilities. Cookware and gourmet shops and mail-order businesses need staff in the kitchen or in packaging or sales.

A socialite who liked to cook and did it well amused her friends when she told them she and her husband would hire out as "the most expensive couple in Beverly Hills" if his job as an aerospace executive evaporated in a periodic recession. "I'm a better cook than most who work for those outrageous salaries in the houses where we go to parties," she said. "Henry can put on his tuxedo, drape a towel over his arm, and pour the wine as well as any butler. And we get to live free."

She wasn't forced into domestic service, but her remark demonstrates the changing status and compensation of household workers, and the cook and butler usually are the best-paid posts on the staff.

Hiring out in a cooking job or food-related job is an excellent way of finding out if you really want to be in the business. You may find you love the hustle and bustle of a restaurant kitchen—or that you detest it! Better to find out before you sink your life savings in a cooking business or get so deeply involved that it is difficult to change to another field.

Working for pay is also a way to learn about the business. Expect to start at the bottom, even if you're a culinary genius at home. But advancement is fast for the dedicated worker. District managers for some of the fast-food restaurant chains are young women and men who began as dishwashers or fry cooks when they were in college to supplement skimpy allowances. Sybil Henderson, who works as a food merchandising consultant in Los Angeles, started as a store demonstrator when she was divorced in the 1950s, had two children to feed and clothe.

As a demonstrator in supermarkets, Mrs. Henderson was so successful at stimulating sales of fresh pears that a regional pear merchandising representative hired her full time for the season. Other commodity groups employed her at other seasons for in-store promotions, supervising demonstrations, and preparing point-of-sale materials. "I didn't know the first thing about preparing point-of-sale materials [posters, leaflets, etc.]," she recalls. "I went to a printer and he showed me how. I went to a home economist and asked her how to prepare food for photography and she showed me." She formed a merchandising firm, specializing in produce. In little more than twenty years she has built her company to full service, including product merchandising and public relations, made Hawaiian papayas and Granny Smith apples from New Zealand market staples, and created markets for other produce items.

Mrs. Henderson still values the face-to-face education of store demonstrations. She thinks her early experience offering tidbits of fresh pears taught her much about consumer reaction. When she had a cranberry account, a demonstrator complained that the customers in an ethnic neighborhood wouldn't taste cranberry relish "because they don't like cranberries." Mrs. Henderson changed the name to Christmas fruit relish and the cranberries almost walked out of the store.

Getting a job in food can be as easy as walking in the door of a restaurant with a sign posted, "Cook's helper wanted," or reading the classified ads in a metropolitan newspaper. *The New York Times* on a slow summer Sunday listed more than fifteen ads for restaurant staff, some jobs requiring experience, but some for the inexperienced.

Some enterprising cooking- and consumer-oriented people write a good résumé and ask for a job. If you are switching careers or reentering the job market after several years as a homemaker, analyze your assets and how they will help you handle a job. Stress your strong interest in foods, naturally.

Efficient management of a household budget and working to organize volunteer projects can help you develop managerial skills. Briefly describe any experience such as these. Also list your education and any work experience, with dates and responsibilities of each job. It is not necessary to give age, marital status, sex, or race on a résumé, though you may give such information if you wish. A résumé should be neatly typed with your name, address, and telephone number in the top left-hand corner. Paragraphs should be spaced to make it easy for a prospective employer or personnel officer to scan the résumé quickly.

Mail or deliver your résumé to a restaurant manager, a supermarket personnel office, a school or food-demonstration service. A covering letter should express enthusiasm, such as, "I like to cook and I can do a good job for you!" Make an appointment for an interview a few days later—and hope. If you're serious about a job, don't be afraid to try something new, advises Sybil Henderson. The turnover of personnel in the food-service industry works for you. A person dedicated to making a career in restaurant, fancy-food manufacture, or catering is almost sure to find a job. Also, due to rapid turnover, promotion can be fast.

Chapter 10
How to Get Paid
to Write about Food

Food writing, whether magazine or newspaper articles, cookbooks or individual recipes, provides a profitable outlet for a culinary interest if you have a knack for putting clear sentences down on paper. Writing is less risky than going into business, requires almost no capital, just a typewriter and kitchen available for recipe testing, and little expense, just food for testing, paper, pencils, envelopes, and postage for submitting manuscripts. You can write part time while a toddler naps, children are in school, or after a day at the office. Or you can make a full-time career of writing. Your schedule is pretty much up to you.

Writing and selling an article or other manuscript can give you a wonderful sense of accomplishment. But you won't make as much money as, perhaps, in a successful mail-order or retail food business. The fame of a by-line in a national magazine may not compare to the thrill of seeing a restaurant flourish and the satisfaction of seeing a bank account or business grow, with you as the mastermind.

A writer must exercise the sternest self-discipline. You must get at the job of testing and writing religiously, as if you punched a time clock at a plant. If you think you can write about food, take these twelve simple steps:

1. Study the market. Read every magazine and food section you can, closely observing recipe types and styles.

2. Analyze the publications, observing the articles and recipes they publish. Take notes on each magazine, noting its interests. Some magazines publish party and exotic food ideas, others deal with everyday foods.

3. In a notebook or on file cards, write the name of the managing editor, articles editor, or food editor and the address of each magazine that publishes the sort of articles that you think you can write well.

4. Below is a list of some markets for food articles. Find out as much as possible about publications that publish your type of articles and recipes. Write the editor, asking if the magazine or newspaper purchases food articles. Usually the editor in charge of purchasing food manuscripts will send you a form letter that might say that the magazine "no longer" or "rarely" or, in fact, "frequently" purchases food articles. The letter may provide other information, such as preferred length, payment, and terms of payment. Some magazines pay for an article on acceptance, some on publication. Usually a letter to an editor is more effective than a telephone call. Letters provide reminders that can be filed for future reference or discussed with other editors in the office.

5. Plan a food article, a subject, and recipes that you think will appeal to the editor or a certain publication (or, in some cases, several publications). Organize your ideas, but don't start to write the article yet.

6. It is not required, but writing a proposal or query

may save you from working up an article that is of no interest to an editor. If you are selling an idea for a book, a proposal is essential to get an advance before the manuscript is written.

A proposal for an article or a book should explain briefly but clearly the main idea of your work: "Mama's Best Recipes for Today's Busy People," "How to Entertain on a Budget," or "Everything You Wanted to Know about Tomatoes—But Didn't Know Whom to Ask." The proposal should express your enthusiasm for the subject, how you will develop it, and how you amassed this knowledge of mama's recipes gone modern, budget entertaining, or tomato enjoyment. Then list the recipes with brief descriptions that you plan to use. For an article, suggest that you can supply fifteen recipes, or whatever number seems appropriate. For a book proposal, you also should list your credentials. Publishers by necessity consider an author's sales potential, which can include a recognizable name or writing credits. Any published articles should be listed. A book proposal should also include your evaluation of who will buy the book and why it is timely.

Study your proposal critically and rewrite it if it seems weak. Also check it carefully for any careless errors and correct them. The purpose of the proposal is to tempt the editor to part with money for your proposed manuscript and to give a clue to your writing ability. You'll find out more about a book proposal later on in this chapter.

7. Mail the proposal—to one editor, if the idea is tailored specifically to one magazine or newspaper. But some ideas are suitable for several. You can send a proposal to several editors, then accept the best offer. It is unethical to send a completed article to more than one editor at a time.

8. You may get a letter in return, "I'm sorry, but this

does not fit our present needs," or some other form of polite refusal. Or you may get a nibble at your bait. The editor may ask for the article on speculation, which means that you will be paid only if the article is accepted. Otherwise, it will be returned to you, and you are then free to submit it to another publication. Or the editor may agree to payment on delivery or publication purely on the strength of your proposal.

9. Write the article, adhering as closely as possible to the writing style of the magazine. Draw your major ideas together in the first few paragraphs—the "drool copy," some editors call them. Remember, these first paragraphs sell the idea of the recipes. However, the opening paragraphs may be sharply edited for space or other limitations. Don't feel insulted if your original priceless prose is greatly abbreviated in print. But don't stint on those first paragraphs either, hoping to outsmart the editor's blue penciling. Make sure your recipes are written in an orderly style and that they are correct.

10. To write a recipe, list each ingredient in the order in which it is used. Use standard measurements or market units, such as a "one 16-ounce can tomatoes." Write the method as clearly as possible, making sure you say "stir" when that is the way the flour is mixed in or "beat" when that is the proper procedure. Give the correct pan size, or a range of sizes, if workable. For baking, specify the oven temperature and provide an estimated cooking time on top of the stove or in the oven or broiler. Most important, also provide a doneness test—tender when pierced with a fork, springs back when the top is touched lightly with a finger, etc. Be explicit on how to turn the finished food out of the pan or if it should be served from its baking dish or pan. Make sure you give an estimated number of average servings. A well-written recipe may seem elementary to a skilled writer, but busy editors are turned off by the many recipes that require drastic editing for clarity and order.

11. Type your manuscript neatly or have a manuscript typist do it. Typists usually charge by the page and cost varies in different areas of the country. Edit your copy carefully before typing. You will save expensive retyping. Your name and address should be typed at the top left-hand corner of the first sheet. Single recipes should have your name and address at the top of the first page of each. Start an article sixteen to eighteen spaces from the top of the page and eight to ten spaces from the top of each following page. Manuscripts always are double or triple spaced to allow room for editing.

12. Keep a carbon copy of your article. Reputable magazines and most newspapers keep careful track of manuscripts, but they *have* been lost. If you don't have a carbon copy, run, don't walk, to the nearest copying center and make one or more. However, don't submit a photocopy or carbon unless you mention that you are submitting a copy because it is sharper or for whatever reason. Some editors suspect that you are guilty of multiple submissions if you send a copy.

13. Mail your neatly typed manuscript with a covering letter referring to the agreement on your proposal. If submitting the article without a prior agreement, write that you are offering the article for possible purchase. An editor once published an article, not realizing it had been presented for sale. It is a help to the editor, and to you, too, if you include your phone number. Enclose a stamped addressed envelope for return of the article in case it is not accepted.

Now wait for an answer. You may get a reply in a few days, but you may have to wait two or three weeks. An editor may hold your article even longer if considering it seriously. At rush seasons such as holidays and vacation periods, when staff members are away or work loads especially heavy, the delay may be prolonged. When an article is accepted, you will get an offer of payment, and you may accept it, or refuse it if you think the article will bring a higher price somewhere else. The editor may send a form letter saying, "Thank you for submitting your article, but it does not suit our present needs." Some editors, if interested in the major theme, may write, "I would be interested in purchasing the article if you will provide another recipe in place of——, or eliminate the recipes for ——"; other minor revisions may be asked for.

One writer who lives in Texas says she isn't fazed at all by the rejection slip, except for the personal disappointment. She simply sends the article out that afternoon to another editor, and if all else fails, she sells the article to her local newspaper. However, an article that fails with one editor should be examined, rewritten, and revised if you think it can be improved for submission to another editor.

A recipe or article is salable if it appeals to an editor first, but ultimately it must appeal to the reader. The editor acts for the reader in selecting articles for purchase. Here are some of the criteria for a salable article or recipe:

1.   A recipe with reader appeal reads as if it will taste good. Except for an occasional exotic recipe, time-tested food combinations are most appetizing in print—chicken and rice, beef and pasta, for example.

2.   For most publications, a recipe must use ingredients generally obtainable in most of the country. The average reader is repelled by ingredients that require a gas-guzzling, time-consuming search.

3. The recipe should use a minimum of ingredients without sacrificing quality and interest. Some magazines limit the number of ingredients to eight, ten, or twelve. Other editors insist that each ingredient be functional, do enough for the flavor or interest-value to justify its use.

4. A recipe must be reasonably easy to prepare and its use determines how elaborate it might be. A family supper dish, for example, must be easy and quick enough to tempt a harried woman home late from the office. A special dessert or splurge food might be considerably more elaborate, and there is a spot in any publication for an occasional show-off dish. There are few absolutes. Certain editors catering to sophisticated audiences prefer at least some off-beat, exotic recipes, the more complicated the better.

5. A recipe must suit the market, appealing to the readers of the publication for which it is written. Here is where your expertise in analyzing the type of food articles published pays off.

6. A recipe is highly marketable if it suits the times. Quick but family-appealing recipes are in vogue, since more women work outside the home. There also is strong interest in certain haute cuisines, created by the gourmet and cooking school cults. Lower-calorie, lower-fat, higher-fiber, and a few vegetarian recipes capture the imaginations of some editors. A few years ago when home gardening was a hot ticket, fresh vegetable recipes had ready acceptance. Some ethnic recipes are in—simple European, Chinese, Japanese, and East Indian—if the ingredients can be adapted to foods easily available everywhere. So an ambitious writer can take many directions, and with the right editor make a sale.

7. Recipes without seasonal or holiday themes can be sold most easily, since Christmas, Passover, or Easter come

but once a year. This gives a magazine only a one-time slot for them, and newspapers, not many more.

Original Recipes

The conventional way to "develop a recipe"—the term used to imply that it is created, not copied—is invention. "You make them up?" an inexperienced editor asked his food writers once. Of course you do, unless you want to be accused of the unethical and illegal practice of copying a recipe from another source.

A group of recipes of uncertain origin that you use in your kitchen do not necessarily make a salable article. Every recipe may be from a standard cookbook. Another dangerous source is family or friends who claim steadfastly that they "created" this recipe, or that a forebear brought it across the ocean in her wedding trunk. Half the time you'll find these recipes copied from package labels or cookbooks.

Make it a rule when you snip and snitch a recipe to write down where and when you got it. This prevents inadvertently writing a recipe into an article when it is the property of another writer.

Editors and publishers deplore the flagrant copying of recipes by cookbook and article writers. If caught, this could be your last sale. The risk of legal action is less critical than embarrassment and loss of credibility.

Publishers, editors, and contest sponsors (recipe contestants are notorious thieves, sometimes because they don't know exactly where a recipe originated) spend much time and money trying to spot stolen recipes, but sometimes miss one. If the investigators find your recipe is not original, the recipe is not sold anyway or you've lost the contest.

But you can *start* with your favorite recipes, whatever

their origins. Judith Jones, cookbook editor at Knopf, who has edited James A. Beard, Julia Child, and many of the world's top food writers, said, "Of course, there's no really original recipe. Somebody has done it before. But you don't just copy it. You add your own touch, maybe just a different way of putting it together." And don't copy an extremely distinctive recipe, very easy to identify by an editor and the informed reader.

Professional home economists and food writers use favorite or good basic recipes as foundations for variations. One skilled writer recently wrote an article on custard as a sauce. A custard is milk, eggs, sugar, a dash of salt, stirred over low heat, then flavored. This writer made a distinctive recipe of basic soft custard by serving it over caramel-coated oranges. In another variation, she changed the granulated sugar to brown and flavored the sauce with rum.

A standard meat loaf can become the subject of an article for a professional writer. He or she will substitute a half pound of pork sausage meat for a half pound of the beef in one recipe variation. Another recipe will use a can of corn for color and texture. Another will use milk for catsup as the liquid and incorporate snips of green pepper for color and flavor.

In working out recipes for sale, write down every cupful, teaspoonful, or pinch of any ingredient. Some writers use test sheets (shown below). Others just jot down the recipe with the date of the test. Make sure each ingredient is listed by its precise name, the word for the ingredient that is universally understood. Canned tomatoes and stewed tomatoes are not the same, for example. Write down the name from the label while the can is still in your hand. The common name usually appears on the label below or separated from the manufacturer's trade name.

This is an example of a test sheet that can be typed and reproduced on a photocopying machine. The filled-in portions show measures and notes you jot down as you work. The test sheet can be scribbled on as much as is helpful to you, since it is for your reference only.

RECIPE TITLE: Spring Pea Soup PROJECT: Cold Soups

SOURCE: Jane Grant, Aunt Kitty, my adaptation

Ingredients:		/Test I 3-6-79		/Test II 3-9-79
1 sm. onion, chopped				
(½ c.)	/	OK	/	OK
1 t. butter or marg.	/	OK	/	OK
1 can (10½-oz.)	/	OK	/	OK
condensed chicken	/		/	
broth	/		/	
1 soup can water	/	OK	/	OK
2 c. frozen or shelled	/	OK	/	3 c.
fresh green peas	/		/	
¼ t. mint flakes	/	OK	/	OK
¼ t. seasoned pepper	/	OK	/	OK
½ c. milk or cream	/	OK	/	OK
Salt, if needed	/	OK	/	OK
Mint sprigs, optional	/	pretty	/	
	/		/	

Method: Cook onion in butter in large saucepan until tender but not browned. Add broth, water, and peas. Bring to a boil, breaking apart peas with fork or wooden spoon, if frozen. Turn heat low, add mint flakes and pepper. Cover and simmer 20 minutes or until peas are tender. Purée in blender or food processor, a cup at a time, until almost smooth. A few flecks of peas make texture interesting. Pour into a large bowl, stir in milk and, if needed, salt. Cover and chill several hours or overnight. Serve in chilled soup cups and garnish each with a sprig of mint.

Comments: *Yield:* 4-5 servings
  3/6 too thin, bland   Pan size: 2-3 qt.
  3/9 fresh delicate flavor Temperature: High, to low

Not only must a recipe have an original twist, something of the writer in it, but it must be as foolproof as possible. Try it in your kitchen. Before testing recipes, make sure your range thermostats have been tested, measuring spoons and cups are standard, and mixers, spoons, pots, and pans are similar to those of the average home cook. Taste a finished recipe and have as many friends and family as possible taste it and express opinions. If there is a defect—the dish is too watery, too thick, too spicy, or too bland—try again to correct it. However, some recipes are so far wrong they are not worth fussing with. Don't waste time working on lost causes. Forget the idea and write the tryout off to experience.

To Whom to Sell

Some regional magazines and many newspapers purchase food articles. These are among the national publications that buy food articles:

  Bon Appétit, 5900 Wilshire Boulevard, Los Angeles, California 90036
  Cuisine (formerly *Sphere*), 500 North Michigan Avenue, Chicago, Illinois 60611

Family Circle, 488 Madison Avenue, New York, New York 10022

Gourmet, 777 Third Avenue, New York, New York 10017

Woman's Day, 1515 Broadway, New York, New York 10036

Selling Single Recipes

Some magazines purchase single recipes for use in staff-written articles. Regional magazines, such as *Southern Living* and *Sunset,* and special audience magazines, such as *Farm Journal,* solicit single recipes primarily from their readers. Payment for single recipes may be small, $5 to $10 each by most publications, but can add up if you regularly write down and sell bright ideas you have for changing recipes.

Your local newspaper may buy single recipes or have a "favorite recipe" feature that pays cash. "Favorite recipe" features generally are used to create reader participation, so limited to persons living within the circulation area of the newspaper.

To prepare single recipes for sale, type each neatly on a separate sheet of paper, one side only. You may write a covering letter, offering the recipe for sale. Most publications will accept a batch of recipes in one envelope; however, don't submit more than one "favorite recipe," since food editors think of a "favorite" as only one recipe.

Food manufacturers occasionally buy recipes to use as models for products for sale or to use in advertising or promotion of one of their products. However, such purchases are rare, since the professionally staffed kitchens and research and development laboratories of most manufacturers generally have thought of and tried almost anything an amateur might invent.

Selling recipes by mail might qualify more as a pastime than as a money-maker. A busy person who can grab a few moments here or there, or even a handicapped person with an errand girl or boy to help, can sell recipes by mail. Have a few hundred copies made on a copying machine. Then advertise in the classified section of a publication. We read in one magazine, "Beef and Beer Recipe, $1 with S.A.S.E.," and the address. S.A.S.E., if you don't know, is a self-addressed stamped envelope. Among the magazines in which such ads appear are *Southern Living, Yankee, New York, Esquire,* and *New West.*

A Literary Agent: To Have or Have Not

Most literary agents have offices in cities, with the majority in New York due to the convenience to major publishers. You can locate agents' names in the classified section of the Manhattan telephone directory, or refer to *Literary Market Place,* an annual directory of agents, publishers, and other information, published by R.R. Bowker Company, 1180 Avenue of the Americas, New York, New York 10036. You may find *Literary Market Place* in your local library. Or write the Society of Authors' Representatives, 101 Park Avenue, New York, New York 10016, for a list of agents' names. Both sources list agents in other cities as well as in New York City.

It is easier to get an agent after you have published, so it might prove simpler to try to sell a book or article yourself, sending out proposal letters and/or the finished manuscript scatter-gun fashion, and then, after selling, seek an agent, showing your credits as part of your credentials.

An agent is invaluable in placing a book and may help you find the right market for an article. However, some agents will not represent a new author in selling articles, since the time and contacts in selling an article are as demanding as selling a book, and for much less money. The agent's fee is a percentage of the sales price.

This is what an agent can do for you.

1. Seek the publisher most interested in your work. An agent keeps up with each publisher's recent books, so would know, for example, that a certain publisher has a new menu cookbook and would not be interested in another.

2. Help you get the best price and contract terms.

3. Advise you on the strengths and weaknesses of publishers who make offers on your manuscript. For instance, the agent knows which publishers provide strongest sales support.

4. Suggest how you can improve your book or article, if it is not quite right for the current market.

5. Advise you on whether to submit a completed manuscript or a proposal. Sometimes a publisher will buy on the strength of a proposal.

A proposal on a book usually consists of a description of your idea and the introductory chapter. Some publishers request a few sample chapters. An advance for a contract drawn on the basis of the proposal provides money while you work, but not all beginners can bring off such a windfall, with or without an agent. And don't expect the million-dollar—or even $100,000—advances that you read about in gossip columns. Those are few, so few that they're good gossip. The advance is against royalties, so you won't get additional money until the advance has been recovered. Figure how many copies of a book must be sold before you, the author, make back $100,000, at 10 percent on the first five thousand copies, 12½ percent on subsequent copies, if the book is priced at $12.95.

* * *

Writing is hardly a get-rich-quick scheme, but some diligent food writers make a living of it. Delores Casella didn't have a high school education when she tried writing food articles. Her first sale was to "Recipe of the Week" in her local newspaper for $5. She collected a drawerful of rejection slips before she sold an article to a national magazine. Ultimately she sold two cookbooks, *A World of Breads* and *A World of Baking*, and has had numerous articles published since, supporting herself and her children with royalties and article sales.

Other writers such as Shirley Sarvis and James A. Beard combine writing with consulting, teaching, or lecturing. As consultants, they advise food manufacturers and restaurants on recipes and menus. The combined careers offer more varied activity, as well as better income to the writer.

Selling Your Own (and Other) Books

Some writers publish their own books and sell them by mail, advertising in newspapers and magazines. You contract with a local printer to duplicate and bind the book. Printing and paper are costly, so get realistic estimates before launching such a project. Shop around for a printer, too, contacting any listed in your local and nearby classified sections of telephone directories. The estimates may vary widely, but study samples of the paper and binding proposed in the contracts before you sign away your savings. Check the prices of ads in such publications as Sunday newspaper supplements in areas where you think the book would draw most interest and in regional magazines. Order enough books in the first printing to justify two or three ads and, most important, have one or two pages in the book filled with clip-out order coupons. If the book is as good as you think, buyers will certainly buy additional copies for gifts.

Write into the contract an agreement with the printer to store the plates so they will be available for second and third printings, though there is a charge for storage. Set a realistic price to cover costs and give you a profit, but provide the purchaser fair value for the money. Most self-published books sell for $5.95 or less, sometimes with an added handling charge.

Certain publishers, quaintly called vanity presses, will publish and market a book for a fee. Publishers who specialize in publishing for money advertise in the book review sections of newspapers and a few magazines. Occasionally a vanity press representative visits a city seeking manuscripts and announces his arrival in an advertisement in local newspapers.

A vanity press is a legitimate business and an alternate way of publishing for a writer who is confident that his or her book will sell. However, some writers who've spent thousands of dollars to have their books published maintain that such publishers do nothing for a beginning author and that a really worthwhile book will find a commercial publisher eventually.

Check the agreements with these companies very carefully. Have a lawyer check the contract, too. Ask any former customers you can locate how much help they got from the company in selling the books. You may have to do most of the selling, which can be a frustrating chore for a person whose talent is for cooking and writing. The author who pays to publish through a vanity press does not earn the prestige that publishing in the traditional system brings.

But there is a bright side, too. A book that does well with a vanity publisher may be picked up and published in a new edition with great financial success and the accompanying prestige by a traditional publisher.

Two writers have made giant steps into full-fledged publishing and distribution, along with the diverse problems of doing business in a highly competitive field. Jacqueline Killeen, tired of long hours as publicity director of the San Francisco Institute of Art, edited a restaurant guide, *101 Nights in California*. Her husband, Roy, an architect, designed and illustrated the book. When Mrs. Killeen was unable to get a suitable contract with a publisher, the Killeens had the book printed and sold it themselves. Before long, both the Killeens were in business as 101 Productions, publishing an annual revision of *101 Nights*, similar restaurant guides by writers in other cities, and other books, predominantly cookbooks.

Vicki Lansky, a young mother, and five other mothers coauthored a book, *Feed Me, I'm Yours*, as a fund raiser for the Childbirth Education Association of Minneapolis–St. Paul. The CEA wasn't prepared to handle the flood of orders for the book on feeding small children. Mrs. Lansky and her husband, Bruce, made a business of it, naming their company Meadowbrook Press, and now publish Mrs. Lansky's and other cookbooks. Her second book written to help mothers serve nutritious snacks, *Taming the C.O.O.K.Y. Monster*, was on *The New York Times* bestseller list three weeks after publication.

A food newsletter is another way for a cook with writing skills to express herself or himself. Most newsletters are aimed at sophisticated readers willing to pay $15, $25, or more per year for news of taste trends, wines, restaurants, and related subjects. The editor and publisher need a good nose for news as well as an interest in cooking.

If you're confident you can write a decent food news article and keep in touch with changing tastes, work out a format for your newsletter. If you know layout and graphics, you might design the newsletter yourself or with the help of a printer with a good eye for layout. If not, employ an art director or layout artist, at least as a consultant. The printer can help you find one.

Work closely with your printer on estimating costs. A newsletter must have a quality look, since its best market is among status-seeking men and women with an interest in food and wine. An interested printer can show you samples of paper in a wide range of prices and should print a sample in the type you choose. Drawings are less expensive to duplicate than photographs, and when used effectively they can look as high quality as photos.

Check costs of distribution and maintaining subscription lists. Newsletters may be advertised in book review or food sections of newspapers or some women's magazines, but to develop a large subscription list you may buy mailing lists. Research distribution costs and add that to the subscription price you will charge.

Bookkeeping and Contracts

A writer escapes heavy capital investment, licenses, sanitation inspections, leasing or buying space, and other details of business. However, she or he is not freed of the need for hardheaded bookkeeping. Keep a record of all expenses connected with your work—from the first grain of salt to the last postage stamp. Even the post office will give you a receipt when stamps are purchased by the hundred and mail is sent registered or certified. Save all receipts and note the manuscript or recipe to which the expense is applied. Have a competent accountant advise you on which expenses are deductible and all the other details of figuring your income tax.

Remember, all repairs on your typewriter probably are deductible, but not all repairs on kitchen equipment if it also is used for preparing family meals. The portion of travel that is necessary for research or appointments with your publisher, CPA, or lawyer can be deducted, in most cases, but don't assume so. The Internal Revenue Service insists on proof that the trip was necessary for a specific project or article. It is almost impossible to qualify for travel and many other expense deductions until after you have sold your first manuscript.

Most writers consider it wise to have an attorney review contracts. Your legal needs probably will not require a lawyer on retainer, but you should establish a business-like relationship with one who will handle problems or refer you to a specialist in the field, when needed.

Many writers, such as Winifred Cheney of Jackson, Mississippi, don't pretend to support themselves with their craft. Mrs. Cheney started writing as therapy when she was recovering from injuries in an automobile accident. She wrote articles for the *National Observer*, which has discontinued publication, and *Southern Living*, and had a book, *The Southern Hospitality Cookbook*, published. She proudly admits she has enjoyed every minute of her part-time career, the recipe testing, the writing, and the people her food writing has brought into her life, but she also enjoys the freedom to spend time with her home, her husband, children, and grandchildren.

The person who makes a career of writing will often be glued to the kitchen range and the chair in front of the typewriter many hours a day, especially when on a deadline. But it allows more flexibility than almost any other phase of cooking for profit. You can work night and day for weeks, meet your deadline, then spend a few weeks exploring an intriguing corner of the world until your next project comes along.

Chapter 11

How to Win
Cooking Contests

Thousands of women, men, and teenagers enter cooking contests every year. A few hundred reach the finals, winning an all-expense-paid trip and sometimes other prizes, as well as a chance at the big money. Only a handful of contestants come home with big prize money—and the winning recipes sometimes mystify also-rans and noncontestants who think they could have easily won $25,000, $10,000, or the prize bag if they had entered the contest.

"I don't see how that woman from Michigan got $25,000 for that pie. Mine is ten times better, and my family doesn't like sesame seed, anyway!" or, "My mother ought to enter her apple strudel. Those contest people would go crazy over it!" make small talk at coffee breaks, over luncheon tables, and at cocktail parties when a contest recipe is publicized.

Why did the judges choose the other pie for a prize of $10,000 to $25,000 (top money in the large national contests) and possibly shun an apple strudel just as delicious as your mother's? We asked three representatives of large national contests, the Pillsbury Bake-Off, the National

Pineapple Cooking Classic and the National Chicken Cooking Contest. They shrugged their shoulders, expressing as much dismay as the public feels about top prize winners. "You tell me!" said Louis Gelfand of Pillsbury. "You've been there!" replying to coauthor Voltz who has judged almost every continuing national cooking contest and many other periodic contests. The judges have complete control over the decision, agreed Ford Worthing, vice-president of Allen and Dorward, Inc., a public relations firm that manages the pineapple cooking competition and, in alternate years, the Professional Pineapple Cooking Contest open to persons in the food-service industry, and Susan Orr, director of the chicken contest.

Sponsors of these and other national cooking contests such as the Men's Pork Cookout Contest, sponsored by the Pork Producers Council, select panels of judges from all areas of the country, usually newspaper or magazine food editors and consumer service directors of supermarkets, in the hope that they will represent a broad cross-section of food tastes and concepts of recipe appeal. (More later about how a judges' panel works.) Food contests are conducted for the publicity they stimulate for the sponsoring group and to produce a prize-winning recipe that is interesting enough to be published and that will tempt consumers to try it. The Bake-Off entry blank for the 1978 contest spelled out criteria simply: "Your recipe will be judged on the following: excellent taste and appearance; quick and easy preparation time and method; popular appeal of ingredients and flavors to stimulate interest in trying the recipe; and good value/cost for the serving occasion."

How to Become a Finalist

The first step to big money is reaching the finals, and many cooking contest hobbyists have participated in the finals of almost every cooking contest and stoutly maintain they don't want to win. They enjoy the game more than winning, and most contests disqualify first-prize winners from future contests. One Pillsbury Bake-Off had more than thirty previous finalists among the one hundred contestants participating, most of them enjoying renewing contest friendships more than striving nervously for the top prize.

A finalist is rewarded with an all-expense-paid trip, usually lavish entertainment for a few days. In the case of the biennial pineapple contest, each finalist and her husband or wife, daughter, mother, or friend is given a tourist's dream week in Honolulu at the luxurious Royal Hawaiian Hotel, as well as one day at a kitchen range cooking his or her entry two or three times, for judges, display, and in case one goes wrong. Each Pillsbury finalist is given $100 spending money in addition to full expenses at the contest hotel and gala dinners by Pillsbury officials and other cooperating sponsors. Finalists in the Men's Pork Cookout Contest are accompanied by their wives to the contest city. The finalists in the chicken contest, usually held in an area where there are active members of the sponsor, the National Broiler Council, have visited Tampa, Birmingham, Jackson, and Charleston with a husband, wife, or other guest, getting the red-carpet treatment wherever they go. Lawry's Foods, Inc., conducts periodic contests for recipes using their many products, from seasoned salt to the newest sauce mixes. This contest, small compared with Pillsbury and other longtime nationals, invites a few finalists to see Los Angeles in the best possible way. The contestants are headquartered at the lastest, flashiest hotel, dine in one or more of the Lawry's restaurants, and have local Lawry's men and women as sight-seeing guides. The cooking, judging, and awards ceremonies take place in the Lawry's Center test kitchen, a southern California–Mediterranean style office building-plant surrounded by a blossom-filled garden. Each contestant gets a gift certificate for the unique gift shop at the center.

So the life of a contestant may be short—but it is sweet to the hobbyists who work for it constantly. Thousands, maybe millions, of recipes are submitted to contests annually. Sponsors usually hire an outside company to sift through recipes first. From the entire batch of several thousand for such contests as the Bake-Off, perhaps half will be eliminated on first reading. "Read the rules," advises Gelfand, "and follow them to the letter." Some recipes don't contain the ingredient required for entering. Some are disqualified because they have been previously printed or been winners in other contests. And many are disqualified simply because a full name and address are not given.

Pillsbury contracts with an accounting firm to screen recipes. The CPA firm in turn employs home economists to screen recipes. In the chicken cooking contest, cook-offs are held in some states to choose finalists. Recipes from other states are screened by a panel of home economists, as are entries in the pineapple contest. The three big national contest sponsors then kitchen test a certain number of the recipes to choose the finalists. Meanwhile, all recipes are coded so the preliminary judges will not be swayed by regional chauvinism, a chance recipe from a friend or relative, or any other personal bias. Recipes are screened, too, to make certain they meet contest criteria.

For the Pillsbury contest the screening organization chooses about twenty-five hundred recipes for consideration as finalists. These recipes, still coded, go to the Pillsbury home economics staff. Any recipes that obviously won't work, seem too elaborate or too common for general appeal, are eliminated on reading. Several hundred are prepared, and the ones that show greatest promise are tested two or three times. Though the contest rules give easy and quick preparation and good value for the serving occasion as criteria, a few more complicated recipes, costly by the home economists' standards, may be included to give choices to the finals judges.

The chicken and pineapple contest officials also conduct preliminary cooking tests to choose finalists. They, too, attempt to provide judges a variety in the styles and tastes of recipes in whittling down thousands to the fifty-one that the chicken contest invites as finalists, forty for the pineapple contest.

Pillsbury carves down the recipes to one hundred, with a few alternates. The pineapple contest sponsors have alternates, too. The chicken contest home economists select an alternate from each state, since there is a finalist from each state and the District of Columbia. A finalist will decide she or he cannot accept the award—the time is not right, illness, or for other personal reasons. In such cases, the alternates are brought into the finals.

The habitual returnees are a mystery to contest sponsors as well as the repeat finalists themselves. "It's knowing how to write a recipe," said one contest sponsor. An illegible or incomplete recipe obviously will be discarded on first reading, but some poorly written ones make the finals in every contest I've (Voltz) judged. The recipes then are rewritten for publication.

A contestant who was a repeater in the Bake-Off finals several years said, "It's in making up a recipe that's just a little tricky, but not too off-beat, then tacking on a catchy name." Her first statement may be true, but Pillsbury and some other contest sponsors often change recipe names to make them more interesting or descriptive or otherwise suitable for print.

How to Win the Jackpot

The finalists in most national contests have reached the cooking area through their description of what they will cook. A recipe contest now becomes a cooking contest. Even more difficult, the contestant is cooking in a ballroom with press and TV cameramen milling around. The room may be warmer than your home kitchen, so bread rises too fast, or it may be cooler, so bread rises too slowly. One Pillsbury contestant in the 1950s had terrible problems: The supermarket whipping cream provided by Pillsbury food shoppers didn't whip up as beautifully as the cream from her own cow at home. Once in Honolulu apples had to be brought in from the Mainland by a contest official when no apples were available in markets in the islands.

One food editor, a good home cook, once remarked while judging, "It's too bad these people don't know how to cook. This would be delicious if it weren't overbaked, and that is just awful, just because he can't cook it."

While the contestants are cooking and chopping, peeling and mixing, for the $10,000 to $25,000 in a hotel ballroom or convention center arena, the judges are closeted in a room nearby. Contest sponsors are so sensitive to possible charges of collusion from contestants or the press that nobody except a person to provide water, freshen coffee, and other palate-cleansers and present the contestants' foods is allowed in the room. Most sponsors post a security guard at the door.

A representative of the contest meets with the judges

in advance and outlines the criteria on which recipes are to be judged. This usually follows the criteria listed on the entry blank. Some sponsors emphasize that they want a recipe that uses the product well, and sponsors of the chicken contest usually say they prefer a recipe that "looks like chicken," though several recent winners have used chicken pieces cut in strips or chunks.

Judges are given copies of the recipes, still coded so they cannot identify contestants. Usually judges are divided into teams, with two tasting each division or, in the chicken contest, two tasting twelve to fifteen recipes. Judges usually rate recipes as they prefer, by scores or simply "first," "second," "third," and so on, adjusting ratings as later entries come in. Some sponsors ask that score sheets be turned in, but judges may prefer to fill in score sheets after all dishes are on the judging table. The judging panel usually includes an odd man or woman, who is captain. She or he votes as a tie breaker for teams who can't make up their minds, and brings the six, eight, or ten best dishes for a final vote by all judges.

Rarely does any one judge taste the one hundred dishes that come into the judging room or the fifty-one chicken concoctions or forty main dishes, breads, salads, and desserts in the pineapple contest. But a conscientious judge tastes as many as half the dishes. How does one have a taste bud left? An experienced taster never *eats*, no matter how good a dish may be, but tastes delicately first, then maybe takes a heartier bite for a potential winner. The palate is cleared by a sip of water, unsweetened coffee, iced tea, or by crunching on a celery stick before tasting another dish.

Potential winning entries are kept on warming trays, or there is a microwave oven in the judging room to reheat them so that they can be retasted when all the dishes are in and the decision to award a pot of money is up to six, eight, or ten people. Disagreements erupt and judges reread the criteria, reread the recipes, ask, "Would you go to the trouble to make this?" or, "Do you think your readers would be disappointed in this? Mine would." Judges talk over the recipes. "I think this is too expensive for what you get." "This seems like piling convenience food on top of convenience food. It takes more time to open the packages than to make a cake from scratch!" "This is just too expensive for a little family dessert. That one is expensive, but you would serve that for a party!"

The final decision may be quick and snappy—by unanimous agreement that a certain dish is a standout and agreement with the judging teams on their best-of-class and seconds awards. Other judges taste prize recipes in all categories, as a rule. If there are strong disagreements, the captain then may ask for secret ballots to choose a winner.

But in dozens of contests, I (Jeanne) have sat in a judging room long past bedtime or the gala "work's-done" dinner while one judge hung the jury and the rest of us would not bow to what we considered a recipe with poor consumer appeal or that was improper for other reasons.

In every way, the last hundred, fifty-one, forty, or fifteen recipes in a contest are as unpredictable as choosing the Triple Crown Winner two years from now by horse-racing fans.

These are the rules to follow—and hope and pray a lot, if you're into contests for money:

1. Read the entry blank and contest rules carefully. Note especially the judging criteria.

2. Play around in your kitchen, using the ingredients required for the contest. Get your family's opinion of

which versions of recipes or which recipes taste best. But write down all of them. The one you least expect may catch the judges' eyes and taste buds.

3. Write down the recipe as clearly as you can, following a model in a magazine or good cookbook if you're not sure how to express a procedure or name an ingredient.

4. Reread the entry blank and make sure you fulfill all rules.

5. Write your name and address legibly in the proper place on the entry blank and, as required, on your recipe. If you can, type your recipe, but a legible handwritten recipe is accepted by all contest sponsors.

6. Mail your recipe, making sure it is on time, several days before the deadline, if possible, to beat any mail delay.

7. If you are chosen as a finalist, take advantage of an offer to try the range you will use in the contest. This offer usually is at a nearby appliance dealer's store. And by all means, try your recipe again.

8. If you have any questions concerning ingredients, a special baking pan, or serving dish, telephone or write the contest sponsor. Some contests encourage bringing your serving and display accessories, such as miniature umbrellas or artificial flowers. Others discourage embellishments such as these.

9. Pack appropriate play and dinner clothes, as well as something cool and comfortable for the cooking floor, usually hot from TV lights and the numerous ranges heating the room.

10. While cooking, be as calm as possible. You'll be interrupted by reporters, writers, and cameramen. It is a good idea to check off each ingredient as you add it to the bowl and to set a timer to remind you when to start, stop,

and bring your food from the oven—triumphantly, you hope.

How to Find a Contest

The national contest sponsors, such as Pillsbury, the Pork Producers Council, the Pineapple Growers Association, and National Broiler Council, advertise their contests in newspapers or magazines. Their entry blanks also are available at the service center in many supermarkets or may be included in packages of their products.

The Lawry's contest is advertised in the regional sections of some magazines, and entry forms are distributed in markets. A New England Apple Cooking Contest was promoted through a television show several years ago. The Cowbelles, an organization of beef producers' wives, sponsors a beef cooking contest, promoted primarily by state chapters. *Woman's Day* magazine organized the James Beard Creative Cookery Recipe Contest twice in the 1970s, highlighting participating advertisers' products, ranging from such varied products as Malcolm Hereford's Cows to Old El Paso Mexican-style foods and Wishbone salad dressings. These contests were advertised in *Woman's Day*. The contestants never cooked for judges. The top recipes were prepared in the *Woman's Day* test kitchens for the judges' tasting. Many newspapers offer prize money for recipes printed in supplements or for "best-recipe" features. These require no cooking by the contestants.

What Fun, Win or Not!

Recipe and cooking contests don't yield great sums of money. It is improbable that anybody will win the $25,000 first prize in the pineapple classic and then one of the

$25,000 prizes in the Bake-Off. But one woman in her sixties, cooking for her eighth time in the Pillsbury finals, had enjoyed every trip and sold and given away enough ranges, awarded as part of a finalist's prize, to feel richly rewarded.

Learning to win can be as satisfying as going out to a job. "Your family thinks you're more important," said one repeat finalist. "My son was telling his friend last week, 'Mom's too busy. She's a Pillsbury winner!'" The press notices, your face on television, even amid an ocean of other faces, can be as exciting as winning an Oscar, and as important to the woman or man who adores cooking and has a creative touch with a recipe.

Grandma's strudel, requiring, as it does, two hours to stretch the dough tissue thin, may not be today's contest style. But her granddaughter's apple muffins may be, and grandma is baking up to date, too. One year I saw a great-grandmother baking an updated sugar coffee cake. This was her first time at the Bake-Off and she was reveling in every minute of it.

Chapter 12

The Bottom Line: What You Need to Know about Finance

One of the most disconcerting experiences that may face a young business occurs when the sales are perking along fine, customers seem happy, even complimentary, but you are losing money or making only a tiny profit that will hardly show up on the year's tax return.

What is going wrong? Perhaps your prices are not high enough to cover the overhead and material costs. Several products in your line might be costing more to produce than you charge for them. You might be overstaffed or not using your employees' time efficiently.

There are hundreds of things that can go awry. And the measure of your enterprise's rightness or wrongness is definite and clear: the amount of money you keep after the bills and employees are paid, the profit.

Learning Experience

According to a survey of new business failures by Dun and Bradstreet, the main reason small firms go out of business is incompetence. The other three major factors were, in order: unbalanced experience, lack of experience in the line of work, and little managerial experience. Incompetence accounted for the failure of 41 percent of the firms and the other three causes for about 50 percent. All four, it should be noted, involve some aspect of work experience. The owner of a specialty-food store was astonished at her own ineptness when she first opened. She recalled: "It takes time before things fall into place. You should have funds to carry yourself and your business for a minimum of three months. It takes at least that amount of time to understand your business and know what the turnover is going to be."

Time does heal the wounds of inexperience but there are ways in which a person starting a business can gain more information about future work. One of the smartest moves is to get a job in the field. If a restaurant is in your future, do a bit of moonlighting as a waiter. You will see how a commercial kitchen operates, the difficulties of dealing with customers, and have a taste of the hours involved running a restaurant. You might have second thoughts. Mrs. Ronald Kemerley, a successful home baker from Arlington, Ohio, found a job in the bakery department of a department store before she ventured out on her own. Some experts recommend that anyone planning to do mass cooking of any kind work in a day-care center or any large food facility. You will learn much about management, nutrition, bulk buying, and short cuts in food preparation.

In urban areas, there usually are night courses for adults at local colleges and sometimes at high schools (if there is no budget or other crisis, as often happens these days). You can bone up on management, accounting, money and banking, and other business subjects for minimum fees. You do not have to pursue a degree or look to become a certified public accountant. You merely study to expand your business expertise. Specialized commercial classes might be available. Ellie Siegel, the underground baker, invested $150 in two classes given by a nationally known pastry chef. She has more than made her money back. She learned to make difficult products, like puff pastries, that were beyond her before. "You can read a million books and you won't get it," she said. "You have to be shown how to do it." One home cook paid one of her young helpers to take a bookkeeping course so that she could dump her accountant.

Incidentally, the three final causes of failure cited in the Dun and Bradstreet study—neglect, fraud, and disaster—amounted to less than 4 percent of the cases. This indicates that the small-business owner is a hard worker, dedicated to his budding enterprise, and that unexpected events such as fraud and disaster play little part in his inability to succeed. But this also would seem to show that an incompetent, inexperienced entrepreneur has slight chance of succeeding, no matter how dedicated and hard working.

How a Business Goes Wrong

Poor decision making can kill a business. You invest all your money in a new line of goods that seems a sure seller—and isn't. You expand too quickly. You invest in new equipment that is supposed to bring in extra cash or effect huge operational savings—but does not. Suddenly, you are a victim of that dread but common ailment of small businesses: cash crisis. You need a quick injection of money or you're out of business. As *Changing Times*, the consumer advisory magazine, has pointed out, the margin for error is slim in a small business. Unlike a large corporation, it does not have the resources to absorb many mistakes. "These independents don't get three strikes before they're out," a management consultant said. "They usually have to hit a home run on the first pitch."

With retail operations, one of the prime reasons for troubles is location. Well-traveled retail sites, such as shopping centers, are likely to be too expensive for a new business. On the other hand, run-down sections of a community are cheap but unattractive to the public. Check the flow of pedestrian traffic, and don't be misled by numbers. The people might be hurrying to a bus stop or the street might be a short cut. Neither type of pedestrian is likely to linger to look in a shop window or study a restaurant menu posted in the window. The ideal location is near large places of employment where people have spare time during the lunch hour or tend to drop in after work.

A common error among small-business owners is buying equipment they do not need: a fancy cash register for a store, a commercial mixer for an incipient home chef. The best way is gradually to purchase secondhand equipment, preferably out of cash receipts from sales. A home cook on Long Island waited nearly a year until she could afford a range that could bake twenty-four pies at a time, then, as the money came in, added a second freezer and a machine press to cut dough into shape. Jeffrey Perlman, partner in Party Box caterers of New York City, remembers one of the initial problems with the business resulted from the expense of the cooking equipment. "It should have been leased," he said. "The idea in this business is not to use your own money. You lease the equipment or borrow the money, if you can."

Watching Finances

One way to figure the cost of keeping an enterprise going is to look at the operating expenses as a percentage of sales. That is, the cost of rent, wages, supplies, etc., as compared with the amount of sales. In prosperous urban areas the average cost of overhead can run as high as 30 percent of sales. This means that every dollar in sales costs 30 cents to produce. Retail operations involving food are among the most expensive for overhead, according to America's Barometer of Small Business. Restaurants, because of heavy personnel and rental costs, and bakeries, which pay heavily for supplies, equipment, and rent, top the list.

The home-run business escapes the major overhead items—rent and, often, wages—and several other expenditures common to the small business. As the proprietor of a kitchen, you can start small and avoid risking a large investment. You only need enough money to buy ingredients for a few pies or whatever you hope to sell. And as a housewife stuck in the home anyway, you do not have to make a profit right away. Initially, you are investing only your time and effort.

Mrs. Ronald Kemerley, who lives in the farmland south of Toledo, in Arlington, Ohio, used her own oven for six months, baking a dozen or so pies a week until her home-baking service became large enough to warrant installing a second one. At first, she made just enough to pay for her groceries. By starting slowly and not being concerned with immediate profit, she was able to ensure that her products—cookies, cinnamon and pecan rolls, German chocolate cakes—were of a quality that satisfied her. She has since attracted a roster of regular customers in the vicinity and added a line of pies. Now she has built a summer market in two nearby campgrounds. She drives through one in a truck, retailing her foods on the spot. At the other, she drops her goodies off at a camp store. She now bakes and sells several pies a day, plus fifteen dozen cupcakes and cookies each and her specialty, pecan rolls. Over the Memorial Day weekend in 1978, she sold ten dozen pecan rolls on her trips to campgrounds.

One of the clichés favored by business advisory services goes that a small firm must keep a backlog of cash, which is as meaningful as saying that for a company to be successful, it must make a profit. Cash is not an easy commodity for a struggling company to have in the house. Credit is another thing. Establishing a line of credit, with suppliers especially, can keep a company from falling over the brink of failure. The marvelous thing about credit is that once established with a respectable company, you can use it as a reference for other loans, taking advantage of the capitalist maxim, "The more you owe, the easier to borrow."

For this reason, loan payments are the last financial obligation to neglect in month-to-month business dealings. Lenders entertain proposals more readily from customers with up-to-date accounts. In addition, to prepare for a possible cash crisis, check to see if you have overlooked any assets. Banks commonly demand security for loans when a business is in trouble. After operating a business for a time, you may well have accumulated collateral of which you are unaware. This might include accounts receivable, that is, money owed by customers; a specialty store could have a valuable inventory; or you might have acquired expensive equipment that will serve as collateral. A loan could be crucial to your survival. Many small businesses, sales bustling, future seemingly bright, have been kayoed by a temporary shortage of cash.

In casting about for financial help, many firms have been saved by taking in a partner with money, an easily workable legal arrangement. One drawback: Lawyers draw a parallel between selecting a business partner and finding a marriage partner. Make the wrong choice and you will rarely have a moment's peace. If you decide to dissolve the union, you'll find that severing a business relationship can be as painful and expensive as getting rid of an unwanted spouse. Loans from relatives sometimes are the only ones available, but these can bring such unwanted disadvantages as forcing you to hire an unneeded nephew or niece and allowing another, often unwelcome, voice in management.

Ironically, business specialists have pointed out that small firms are often too ready to cry "cash crisis." As SCORE, the Service Corps of Retired Executives also known as the "paunch corps," has stressed, "Lack of money, a chronic condition in most small businesses, carries the brunt of the blame for problems, and, often, incorrectly." Proprietors think their needs are "financial when they are actually managerial."

At any rate, despite the complexities and hazards of running a small company, the number of new businesses grows each year. In 1976, 320,000 new firms were started; in 1977, the total swelled to almost 500,000. The rate of failure, however, remains constant. Half of the small firms were out of business in two years, and nearly 80 percent will go under within five years. The 20 percent that make it over the five-year hump encourage others. Some of the companies started in the early 1970s are now fat and secure enterprises.

Watching Costs

One of the handiest tools for rescuing a business in trouble, or making a thriving concern healthier, is cost analysis. Wisely employed, it can reduce expenses and increase sales without ballooning operational costs. Essentially, the process involves rooting out unnecessary expenses and unprofitable products and zeroing in on profitable lines and expanding them.

The guts of cost reduction is sound bookkeeping. You must know the amount of ingredients used in a product, the time consumed in preparing it, and any and all overhead expenses, such as transportation and packaging. Cost reduction does not mean across-the-board cuts. It means analyzing which variable expenses can be eliminated or reduced. By figuring the cost of producing a line of cakes or a fancy casserole dish and comparing it with income from sales, you can judge whether or not the products are profitable or worth the bother.

In scrutinizing expenses, percentages tell more than dollar amounts. Any increase in sales that does not appreciably affect expenses reduces the ratio of expenses to sales, a boon to profits. Conversely, if in order to increase business you must make large capital or operational outlays, the percentage gain in costs might not justify the expansion. It is comforting to know that once an enterprise is making money—once it is paying for rent, salaries, and utilities—these fixed expenses decline as a percentage of volume with every escalation in sales.

Advertising and Promotion

You do not have to spend heavily on advertising. Often a single small ad, display or classified, placed in the proper publication will do the trick. As mentioned, Sam Milliken, owner of the catering concern A Private Townhouse Affair, drew a surprising response with one small, simple ad in *New York* magazine. Around the country, there are many city or regional magazines like *New York* that have a certain cachet among mobile, big-spending singles and young marrieds.

For home-cooked products, the best advertising is word

of mouth. In both small towns and city neighborhoods, people boast about party-going, what the affairs were like, and an outstanding pastry or coquille St. Jacques calls for comment and is sure to get it. A Manhattan resident once was asked if she knew a good caterer. An enthusiastic cook herself, she volunteered and, astonished to see that her cooking talents had monetary value, went into the catering business. Soon word of her abilities spread and she was being hired to cater corporate lunches.

This young woman had a talent for self-promotion. She spent a good deal of time on local talk shows, demonstrating food preparation and discussing special dishes. She once catered for free a benefit at Bloomingdale's, the faddish New York department store. She considered the $125 it cost her for ingredients worth five times that amount in ordinary advertising. Most communities have some delicatessen, food shop, or, as at Bloomingdale's, a unit in a larger store known for its discriminating taste and special products. Getting your home-prepared wares in such an outlet serves as an advertisement in itself.

Become well known in your community. Don't be shy. You are selling a quality product. Notify women's clubs that you can provide cakes, casseroles, or sandwiches for their meetings or social events, and don't be cheap about distributing free samples. Any public affair that draws large groups of people is worth patronizing. In the city, there are block parties, and in the suburbs and small towns, there are yard and garage sales and flea markets. Investing in a table at these affairs as a promotion can bring future sales.

Community newspapers dote on feature stories about local businesses, if the enterprise is in any way unique. In a first job on a small newspaper, one young reporter did features on an inventor of a machine that automatically matched paints, the town's first Chinese restaurant, a chain store that specialized in soft ice cream. You don't have to advertise in the publication first. Even small newspapers try to keep advertising and editorial departments separate, although they are not always successful. Step back and look at your operation and decide what is different about it. The local press was delighted by Mark Mc-Neely, mentioned earlier, and his Just Desserts restaurant for the offbeat products like toffee bars and banana chips that he featured. Kentucky Fried Chicken pushed the southern colonel image of Colonel Sanders so successfully that he became a national figure.

If you have trouble being noticed, package your most special product with a publicity release and an eight-by-ten-inch glossy photograph. Specialty-food producers can send these to the trade magazines for the industry they are trying to reach. If you are in the mail-order business, send the material to the food editors of major metropolitan newspapers and national women's magazines. Simply write "food editor" and the name and address of the newspaper or magazine. For trade magazines, address the label to the new product editor. You can compile a list of media with a visit to your local library. Verify addresses by checking the out-of-town telephone books at your local telephone company in their yellow-page listings.

Package your products in small shopping bags with your name and address displayed prominently. They will be used again and help spread your name. Put some thought and imagination into the design. Department stores have been very successful with this device. Some of their bags are recognizable a block away.

Collections

Some novice businessmen consider collections the touchiest area in business. They do not like sending out bills and abhor the idea of dunning someone for money. Hence, collecting tends to be one of the most neglected jobs in small businesses. But it is as essential to success as bookkeeping and other irksome chores and must be done thoroughly on a regular monthly basis.

Some caterers and sellers of home-cooked products are paid on delivery. One New York City caterer said, "I ask the customer to have a check ready for me in the exact amount. I don't get involved in billing people. The nicest people in the world don't pay their bills." Most small-business men start out taking any job without worrying about cash but after encountering a few problems, they come around to demanding a deposit, normally at least 50 percent. Jeffrey Perlman, of New York's Party Box, commented, "At first, we did anything without asking about money. Not anymore. We're more careful. Usually, it costs more money to take someone to court than it's worth." The firm's most memorable collection hassle came from an unexpected quarter, an immensely respected museum.

A caterer or store with collection problems might consider using one of the major national credit cards. Companies like American Express have offices in all large cities. Contact the sales office to make the arrangements. The company requires a minimum volume from the retailer, but that's flexible and can be discussed with a sales representative. If you are eligible, the credit card company will work out a contract and provide you with an imprinter to process the sales slips. The negative kicker: The service charge is 3 to 5 percent, depending on volume.

Advice on Taxes

An extraordinary array of living costs become tax deductible when you are in business for yourself. The home-based business offers even more tax benefits. To justify any type of deductions, you must keep records that reflect your business activity. Set up your books so that income and expenditures for personal transactions do not get mixed in with business matters.

One of your first steps in starting a business anyway should have been to open a business checking account. This not only keeps your personal money separate from your business money, but the information you need for your bookkeeping system is taken directly from your checking account records. Your accountant should figure out your deductions, but it is your job to provide him with complete records. Some guidelines:

Avoid cash payments for business supplies. If you must, get a cash receipt for the smallest item. Checks are preferable.

Make certain that your household records show the amount paid for bills connected with the business. These include insurance, tax payments, even the electricity and gas consumed in cooking. For the home cook, this can be difficult.

Keep your records after filing your annual federal income tax. Experts recommend holding them for seven years to be safe.

Pricing Your Wares

Calculating the correct price for your cooked or baked goods is the most ticklish decision in business. Even the professionals disagree here. Obviously, the price must cover production to make a decent profit. Or not so obviously. Some home cooks fail to put a proper value on their time and end up undercharging. That's all right to build a market, but not as a policy. Most successful home cooks employ a rule of thumb. Unfortunately, the thumb keeps changing size. They total the cost of the ingredients and double or triple the figure to arrive at the selling price. Some even quadruple the cost of ingredients. You will have to discover the method that works for you, one that gives you a satisfactory amount of money and does not scare away buyers. Caterers have it relatively easy. They can estimate cost per guest and add a reasonable profit for a night's work. Keep in mind that there are four elements involved in calculating the best selling price: (1) material and labor; (2) production overhead, rent, or building costs figured down to a weekly or daily rate, other ongoing expenses such as utilities; (3) nonproduction costs such as your salary and delivery; (4) profit. Profit should be figured at a minimum of 25 percent, because of the slow seasons and other vicissitudes of food service.

If your product is rejected as being too high priced, you can experiment with less costly ingredients. But the irrefutable fact is that the quality of home-cooked products depends on using the best ingredients, and quality is what you are selling. Price, as mentioned earlier, is not that crucial a factor in home-prepared goods, as long as your prices are not fantastically high.

General Tips on the Food Business

A caterer can check out interesting locations for banquets and parties in the area. Food's attraction always is enhanced by the environment in which it is served. Sam Milliken, proprietor of the townhouse catering firm, owes much of his reputation to his plush Manhattan headquarters, the former Bulgarian embassy. The townhouse gimmick has worked so well that he now has a list of private Manhattan townhouses, all well appointed, that are available for temporary rental.

You might check the community's parks department. Often, city facilities with kitchens are available for rather moderate rents. Historical landmarks—charming old buildings and municipal white elephants—might welcome a responsible caterer who would bring income to offset maintenance expenses. Offer everything from coffee and Danish to sandwiches and full box lunches to groups using the facilities.

Committee box lunches are a growing fad. Some meetings of government and business executives do not take luncheon breaks, feeling they are too time consuming, if not too fattening and expensive. The town board in one eastern Long Island community regularly receives publicity for their "brown-bag lunches" as a way of showing their dedication to good government. Companies with private dining rooms, too, often need caterers or cooks to supply snacks for private gatherings.

Save coupons from packages. You will be dealing in volume and through a lot of groceries. Like one commercial home baker, you can pile up coupons from something such as a special flour she bought, and use them to acquire for free the silverware, silver trays, and occasional other accessories needed in a catering business, as she did.

Always be alert for ways to save money. For example, as a home cook, even if you are in a service business, you are not necessarily in the delivery business. Encourage customers to pick up their orders from you rather than automatically assuming that you have to deliver. Of course, if the customer insists on home delivery, despite all your efforts to the contrary, you must comply.

Read trade publications. They are available at a public library. In some fields, such as restaurants, there are a dozen or more. Join any trade association connected with your business and subscribe to any publications that seem worth the money. Read library copies of magazines as old as two years back. It will update you on problems or teach you aids you may never have thought of.

Learning to use your nearest large library is smart. The periodical room will contain journals and magazines, and the index to individual articles will be in the *Readers' Guide*. The card catalogue lists books by subject as well as by title and author. Learn the rules of the library, whether patrons are allowed in the stacks (book storage areas) or if a librarian must find a book for you. Periodicals and reference books usually cannot be borrowed from a library but must be read there. Most other books can be borrowed if you obtain a library card.

Exercise extreme care in hiring. Check with your lawyer about your liability. Try to stay with part-time or freelance help. It cuts down on the paper work and the financial responsibility. A temporary or part-time worker does not make you responsible for unemployment insurance, worker's compensation, tax deductions, etc.

Specialized Tips to Build Business

In restaurants, set aside a table in a corner for backgammon groups, embroidery clubs, or card clubs for lunch (but watch out for any wagering—it's probably illegal). Chess is a popular game for play and amusing to watch. A Manhattan restaurant enjoyed great success with a "dutch treat" table for single men who did not like to dine alone.

Set up an omelet bar, a crêpe bar, a build-your-own sandwich bar. It's the same idea as the ubiquitous salad bar, but the diner fills his omelet or crêpes, sauces to taste, and, if needed, an attendant supervises.

Mail-order is a relatively safe method of expanding your market or going into business without making a heavy investment. For home cooks with regional specialties, this method of selling is particularly appealing. Hollister Kent, a noted specialist in land planning, borrowed $1,500 to organize a mail-order house featuring delicacies from his native Vermont. His products ranged from maple syrup to chutney. He solved the key problem in this line of business: the mailing list. He was loaned a card file belonging to his mother, cookbook author Louise Andrews Kent.

In promoting cooking schools, don't forget that today almost as many men as women are interested in expanding their culinary knowledge. And the ethnic trend here is as strong as it is in the rest of the food field. The teaching of Chinese cooking appears to be the latest fad. One Manhattan cooking school operator with an imaginative flair cocked his eye at business people who have difficulty in finding free time on weekends or evenings, the most popular hour for classes. As a service, the school offers a sunrise baking course. It begins at 8:00 A.M. and runs until 8:45 A.M.

American corporations spend more than $1 billion a year on Christmas gifts. Companies look for something different, something memorable that will be commented on. Homemade products fit this description like a glove. They are a far more personalized gift than a commercial product. Contact companies to find out who does the buying. It usually is the purchasing agent, the head of personnel, or the public relations chief.

Watch special occasions. A "new mother dinner" or box lunches, rosebud in a vase, in the hospital—a gift from doting grandparents or husband, of course. Consider other hospital patient meals, where allowed—you might work with the hospital dietitian and have gift shop operators distribute flyers for a small commission.

Obtain free brochures and booklets containing recipes or instructions from manufacturers to give away to your customers. Promotional-minded companies are delighted to supply you with these free items. Cooking schools could take advantage of these materials for students' use and avoid reprinting of recipes and preparation of instructions.

Be ready to experiment. You must move with public tastes and continually try new recipes. It's fine to start with a few favorite dishes, but stand ready to fill any kind of order. You are in a service business. Read ethnic cookbooks to discover foods that are not commonly available. Research the history of any ethnic item that you choose for production or sale. Take a tip from Pepperidge's success and put the history on the back label of a product. This could be especially effective for items that would classify as small hors d'oeuvre, canapés, or appetizers. It makes for "cocktail party" talk.

Closet Cuisine

We have previously mentioned Ellie Siegel (a fictitious name), the home baker who works out of New York City's Upper East Side outside the law. She is one of a multiplying legion of merchandisers of closet cuisine who provide restaurants, specialty stores, and caterers with unique dishes not produced by commercial organizations.

We got an idea of the scope of home cooking when we brought up the subject to a Manhattan housewife who lives on the West Side, an area known for its ethnic food stores and whose residents are famous for jumping on the latest urban fads. She laughed, "I think every woman in this apartment building is cooking or baking something for sale. One of them sells to the restaurant next door and got a visit from the health department. He warned her to stop. He didn't give her a summons, though. She laid off for a couple of months and now she's back at it."

"In this business," Mrs. Siegel says, "you charge for going

to the bathroom." She works steadily for the caterer and gets top dollar for her wares. "Friends call me and order two fruit tarts or say they want four quiches. It adds up. I'm booked for the next five months for parties, making pastries, quiches, mousses, and dips. If you can cook, it's really a big business, particularly if you specialize. I specialize in hors d'oeuvre and baking."

Of course, problems arise now and then. Her apartment kitchen is small and difficult to work in. Her closets are overflowing with bulky baking pans and other pieces of the $1,000 in kitchen equipment in which she has invested. Three young active boys occasionally are in the way of her avocation, sticking fingers into a pie or wiping the icing off a cake. When her youngest was six, he took a tiny nibble out of each of thirty-two cookies she had baked and put aside in the living room. They were ruined. She screamed at him: "Why all of them?" "If I took a tiny bit, I thought you wouldn't notice," he answered logically.

She could go legitimate. An acquaintance wants to underwrite the expenses for a specialty-food store featuring her creations. Another businessman in the food line wants to market her products nationally. But she is content—for now. "Imagine," she said with a grin. "Out of twenty-four brownies—this!"

Is It Worth It?

Underlying the entire at-home cooking fad is the unique satisfaction that a person receives when something he or she created has a commercial value, that it not only sells but provides pleasure to absolute strangers. Ellie Siegel, who started business by baking brownies, enjoys serving at expensive dinner parties as part of her work with caterers. At these affairs, she relishes hearing comments to the hostess like, "My dear, these fruit tarts are priceless. Where did you get them?"

Yet it is hard to listen to her comments on her work and understand how she can exult in what she calls its freedom. One Saturday afternoon she was sitting at her house by the ocean having coffee and chatting about her baking. She had been up since 4:30 that morning because she was nervous about a party she was working that night and could not sleep. She talked of spending fifteen- to sixteen-hour days between her baking and her family and told anecdotes about baking disasters that destroyed hours of careful preparation. (Once a pound cake refused to rise after eight tries and delivery time was getting near. She substituted a marble cake recipe and it worked. Later, she conjectured that an impending hurricane that had lowered the air pressure was to blame.)

Incidentally, she did work the party that night and got home at 3 A.M., we learned the next day. Her husband exploded in anger and forbade her ever to serve another dinner party. We'll see. Her husband now feels that he has created a Frankenstein's monster: He was the one who had urged her to find some kind of work to keep herself busy while the children were at school.

We suspect that what she has called her freedom is a change in attitude. She now values herself as never before. Over the years, she had grown to view herself as just another housewife. She did the cooking and took care of the kids, and that was all she was capable of. Now she has risen in her own esteem. She knows that the caterer depends on her and feels he likes her as much for her outgoing, public personality as for her baking talent. She is proud of her worth. As for the owner of the specialty store, she thinks, possibly wrongly, that without her pastries he would go out of business. At any rate, she considers herself an independent person with a claim to uniqueness, not a nine-to-five office hack.

At a conference held on starting a small business, a speaker described what he thought was the consensus of the meeting, and he could have been talking about women like Ellie Siegel. He declared, "We want to get across that if you can do it in the business world, what better way to achieve self-fulfillment than to go into business for yourself. The thrill is fantastic, absolutely addictive."

Chapter 13
Where to Go for Help

Almost every small business falls on bad times at least once, sometimes several times, before doing business successfully becomes a habit. Your banker, accountant, lawyer, and insurance man are your first rescue team. But many small-business people overlook the good and generous aids offered by public and private agencies. Some of this help to small business is free, some available at a small charge.

These are agencies you should know about in case disaster strikes, and many will give you help in getting a business started:

The local chamber of commerce provides demographic studies and information on the business health of the community and future business opportunities. Some new business people regard membership in the chamber of commerce valuable.

County and state economic development commissions are mandated to develop and assist the development of private business in their regions, so they are a gold mine of information on where and when to locate, what kinds of business can prosper and what types are unsuitable for the area. Some governmental economic development commissions will go so far as to assist an entrepreneur in borrowing capital or expansion money.

Government

Government on all levels is designed to encourage business. Your first contact is the Small Business Administration. (It is listed in the telephone directory under United States Government.) The SBA has a hundred offices throughout the United States and can provide you with basic information on how to operate a small business (see publications list below). The SBA conducts business workshops, short courses on business subjects, and other training programs as well as providing loan assistance.

The federal Department of Commerce also is a fertile source of information on small businesses. Check your local office. States and some cities also maintain commerce departments. Do not forget that your chamber of commerce can be helpful, from advising on loans to furnishing local business contacts.

Some states have education departments that map out study outlines and other materials on a variety of business subjects. Bookkeeping, money management, and management techniques are among the standard courses.

State divisions of veterans affairs can provide assistance. The majority of persons working in cooking services are women, but the number of men engaged in this work is increasing. The veterans' agency has available specially trained counselors to give guidance and assistance on business ventures. Veterans' counseling offices are conveniently located in most counties in all states.

SBA publications run the full gamut of business fundamentals. Write the agency in Washington, D.C., for a list of small-business aid publications. Most are free. A sample of titles: "Analyzing Your Cost of Merchandising"; "Is Your Cash Supply Adequate?"; "The ABCs of Borrowing"; "What Is Your Best Selling Price?" Finally, SCORE and ACE (Active Core of Executives), organizations of experienced executives, work out of the SBA. Their members are available for individual counseling and advice. These agencies are listed under the SBA in the telephone directory.

Trade Associations

Membership in an association of your peers offers many advantages, sharing experiences with others who've had them being one of the most important. These are some trade associations and the services they offer:

Association of Cooking Schools, c/o Don Miller, l'Académie de Cuisine, Bethesda, Maryland 12538. Organized in 1978, this association publishes a newsletter, will publish a directory, and maintains a certification program, based on a point system.

Direct Mail/Marketing Association, Inc., 6 East 43rd Street, New York, New York 10017. This organization maintains a hot line for members where they can get answers to questions about where to go for packaging materials, mail regulations, or how a labeling regulation affects your product. It also offers periodic seminars on various aspects of direct mail in different parts of the country, publishes a newsletter, and organizes an annual meeting.

National Association for the Fancy Foods Trade, 1270 Avenue of the Americas, New York, New York 10019. This organization sponsors two fancy-food shows a year, in various parts of the country. It also conducts seminars on various facets of business in conjunction with the shows and at other times.

National Restaurant Association, One IBM Plaza, Chicago, Illinois 60611. This organization is almost sixty years old and has a large staff. Members pay dues on the basis of volume of business, so for a small restaurateur who uses the NRA services efficiently, membership may be a bargain. NRA offers periodic seminars in various parts of the country, has bulletins and brochures on various aspects of business available, as well as such assistance as accounting systems for small restaurants. The association sponsors two shows annually.

International Food Service Manufacturer's Association, John Hancock Building, 875 North Michigan Boulevard, Chicago, Illinois 60611. Membership consists principally of suppliers of equipment and materials a food business might use, but the entrepreneur in a food business will find the *Encyclopedia of Food Service,* published and frequently revised by the association, invaluable because of the lists of contacts it provides.

National Association of Retail Grocers of the United States, P.O. Box 17288, Washington, D.C. 20041. Representing independent food retailers, this organization provides a variety of services, including store planning and engineering, operational methods and procedures, advertising and merchandising, accounting and record keeping. Some of its activities can be invaluable to new retailers. NARGUS sponsors educational seminars and training clinics. It also publishes booklets, leaflets, manuals covering every phase of food-store management.

Associated Retail Bakers of America, Presidential Building, Suite 250, 6525 Belerest Road, Hyattsville, Maryland 20782. An organization of retail bakers, it produces bread, cake, and other baked products for sale in its own shops. It provides information that can be useful to the small retailer, such as advice on management, food handling, and merchandising. The group circulates a monthly publication to which members can subscribe. Its annual convention is scheduled for St. Louis in 1979 and for New Orleans in 1980.

National Association of Convenience Stores, 5205 Leesburg Plaza, Falls Church, Virginia 22041. This association represents retail food stores with limited stock. These stores are usually open longer hours than supermarkets and charge accordingly. The organization sponsors seminars and has a quarterly newsletter.

International Society of Gourmet and Specialty Retailers. This is part of a profit-making company, unlike the organizations previously listed. Davies Publishing Co., of Hinsdale, Illinois, is the owner. But the organization does offer educational and promotional ideas for the small store. It also is strong on researching trends in the field.

National Association of Food Equipment Manufacturers, c/o Smith/Bucklin and Associates, 111 East Wacker Drive, Chicago, Illinois 60601. This one is for the more experienced or high-volume cooking service operators. It represents manufacturers of commercial food equipment for restaurants, hotels, and institutions. As a small-volume food business, you might have difficulty qualifying, but the association will keep you up on the latest developments in kitchen equipment. It publishes a newsletter.

Metal Cookware Manufacturers Association, P.O. Box D, Fontana, Wisconsin 53125. This is a group of manufacturers of metal cooking utensils and metal cooking accessories (the former Aluminum Wares Association).

Journals and Magazines

Reading current literature informs a business person of the changing styles in his industry. In the food business, caterers, gourmet-food producers, and restaurateurs also keep up with the popular press—the high-fashion shelter magazines such as *House and Garden* and *House Beautiful* as well as the women's service magazines that emphasize recipes and menus. These are some of the periodicals about food that can be helpful. A novice can study them in a public library, then subscribe to the ones that seem best to suit his or her needs.

Food Management, 757 Third Avenue, New York, New York 10017. This is a monthly magazine for the institutional food-service field with articles on topics ranging from menu planning to employee motivation, from food purchasing to legislation.

Catering Executive Newsletter, P.O. Box 788, Lynbrook, New York 11563. Ths is a bimonthly magazine devoted to social caterers.

Good Food, Radnor, Pennsylvania 19088. This monthly gives gourmet tips for the family cook and may be helpful for the small cooking entrepreneur.

Gourmet, 777 Third Avenue, New York, New York 10017. This glossy monthly, with its food- and wine-related tales of personal experiences and adventures, can provide new ideas for the food pro as well as amateur.

California Cookbook Bulletin, 555 Buena Vista W. 405, San Francisco, California 94117. This regional monthly is for people who like the better things in life—like fine food and wine.

Bank of America Small Business Report, San Francisco, California 94137. This publication gives detailed case studies of small-business problems and solutions, and is available at lending libraries.

Other publications: *Cooking for Profit*, Madison, Wisconsin 53711; *Fast Service*, 757 Third Avenue, New York, New York 10017; *Food Service Marketing*, Madison, Wisconsin 53711; *Hospitality*, 633 Third Avenue, New York,

New York 10017; *Institutional Distributors*, 633 Third Avenue, New York, New York 10017; *Nations Restaurant News*, 425 Park Avenue, New York, New York 10021; *Restaurant Business*, 633 Third Avenue, New York, New York 10017.

Cooking Schools

Study with other cooking teachers is an inspiration for cooking school directors, and credits from a well-known cooking school can enhance your prestige. Study in a good cooking school also offers a caterer, specialty-food producer, gourmet shop owner, or small-restaurant operator an opportunity to keep up with food trends. These are well-known cooking schools that offer sound foundations in classic techniques, as well as updated ideas. There are many other good ones, perhaps one in your region.

Julie Dannenbaum's Creative Cooking, Inc.
1816 Delaney Place
Philadelphia, Pennsylvania 19103

Madeleine Kamman's Modern Gourmet, Inc.
81 R Union Street
Newton Center, Massachusetts 92159

La Varenne École de Cuisine
34 Rue St. Dominique
75007 Paris, France

Le Cordon Bleu
24 Rue de Champs de Mars
75007 Paris, France

Going Back to School

Almost every community college system in the country offers courses in chefs', bakers', and restaurant cooks' training, restaurant and catering management, and other technical training programs. Community colleges and adult education programs in colleges, universities, and local school systems offer courses in small-business management, bookkeeping, accounting, personnel, and the many aspects of doing business that a novice may find helpful. Many community education systems offer work-study programs, in which a student can work part time in his chosen field and go to school part time.

A young person, or an older person with time to do it, may choose a four-year college or university program to prepare for a career in cooking. Check your state board of education for the names of colleges and universities in your region that offer degrees in food service. These are among the nationally known colleges and universities in this field:

Cornell University
School of Hotel Administration
Ithaca, New York 14850

Florida International University
School of Hotel, Food, and Travel Services
Miami, Florida 33144

Florida State University
Department of Hotel and Restaurant Management
Tallahassee, Florida 32306

Iowa State University
Ames, Iowa 50010

Johnson and Wales College
Providence, Rhode Island 02903

Michigan State University
School of Hotel, Restaurant, and Institutional
    Management
East Lansing, Michigan 48823

Pratt Institute
215 Ryerson Street
Brooklyn, New York 11205

University of Massachusetts
Department of Hotel and Food Administration
Amherst, Massachusetts 01913

These are among the schools with national reputations in chefs', cooks', and food-service training that offer courses that, when completed, earn a diploma or certificate:

L'Académie de Cuisine
5021 Wilson Lane
Bethesda, Maryland 20014

Culinary Institute of America
Hyde Park, New York 12538

References

Restaurateurs, caterers, fancy-food manufacturers, cooking school teachers, and food writers refer to cookbooks constantly for ideas and to check standard recipe formulas. One or two general cookbooks and as many specialty cookbooks as you like become your cookbook library. Books can also help you over rough spots in business, and these are some:

Blair, Eulalia C. (editor), *Professional Recipe Master* (Hayden)—a spiral-bound collection of classic recipes in large-quantity sizes. Recipes are clearly written, so the book is invaluable to an inexperienced cook, and is an ideal kitchen manual when cooks' helpers must be employed.

Brownstone, Douglass L., *How to Run a Specialty Food Store* (Wiley)—a practical guide, detailing how to keep accounts, buy and receive shipments, and work with staff. This book is aimed at health-food stores, but provides information helpful to any specialty-food shop.

Dahl, Crete, *Food and Menu Dictionary* (Cahners)—an aid in writing menu copy correctly, plus identification of foods with which you may not be familiar.

Dahmer, Sondra J., and Kahl, Kurt W., *The Waiter and Waitress Training Manual*—a well-illustrated guide to the duties of a waiter or waitress, including how to set a table, take and serve an order, and illustrations of uniforms.

Dukas, Peter, *How to Plan and Operate a Restaurant* (revised second edition) (Ahrens/Hayden)—a comprehensive guide to starting and running a restaurant, with ample warnings against pitfalls and mistakes you might make.

Dyer, Dewey A., *So You Want to Start a Restaurant* (Cahners)—the full story, similar to the book above, on how to succeed while really trying.

Handbook of Food Preparation (American Home Economics Association)—recipe-writing forms, basic proportions for standard recipes such as cakes and white sauce, temperature charts for baking and other method of cookery, and purchasing guides to common foods; a help to a writer, editor, caterer, cook in a restaurant, or a gourmet-food manufacturer.

Kotschevar, Lendal H., and Terrell, Margaret E., *Food Service Planning* (Wiley)—a detailed book on skills required in food-service kitchens and dining rooms.

Montagné, Prosper (American edition by Charlotte Turgeon), *The New Larousse Gastronomique* (Crown)—the classic encyclopedia of everything under the culinary sun, a chefs' handbook for almost half a century.

Splaver, Bernard, *Successful Catering* (CBI Publishing)—a manual for the large caterer, with aids for a novice.

Stokes, John, *How to Manage a Restaurant or Institutional Food Service* (William C. Brown)—a scholarly book on operating a large or small restaurant or institutional kitchen.

Weiss, Edith and Hal, *Catering Handbook* (Ahrens/Hayden)—almost anything you need to know, from how to load the truck to how to carve a watermelon.

Index